MW01116142

Keeping the Heart

The Great Work of a Christian

In Modern English

John Flavel

Jason Roth

"Keep your heart with all vigilance,
for from it flow the springs of life."
Proverbs 4:23

Keeping the Heart: The Great Work of a Christian: In Modern English
Copyright © 2020 by Jason Roth. All Rights Reserved.
Revision 20200925
ISBN: 9798672816456

Christian Classics for the Modern Reader

Source text:
A Saint Indeed, or The Great Work of a Christian in Keeping the Heart in the Several Conditions of Life by John Flavel
London: printed by W.R. and sold by Robert Boulter,
at the Turks head in Bishops-gate street, near the Great James, 1670

Translation and annotations by Jason Roth

All rights reserved. No part of this book may be reproduced in any form or by any electronic or mechanical means including information storage and retrieval systems, without permission in writing from the author. The only exception is by a reviewer, who may quote short excerpts in a review.

Cover photo by Evgeni Tcherkasski on Unsplash.com.

Scripture quotations are from the ESV® Bible (The Holy Bible, English Standard Version®), copyright © 2001 by Crossway, a publishing ministry of Good News Publishers. Used by permission. All rights reserved.

Contents

About this Book

John Flavel (1627-1691) was an English Presbyterian minister and author. This book was originally published in 1670 as "*A Saint Indeed, or The Great Work of a Christian in Keeping the Heart in the Several Conditions of Life.*" It is centered around Proverbs 4:23:

> *"Keep your heart with all vigilance,*
> *for from it flow the springs of life."*

Flavel maintains that it is our great responsibility to watch our hearts and guard them against sin and lifelessness in spiritual duties. This watchfulness also results in a more joyful and victorious life that adorns the Gospel with beauty.

Keeping the Heart is an immensely practical book. Flavel first gave the Biblical advice to his congregations before compiling it into the material you read here. The main part of the book provides advice on how to approach various seasons of life that each pose their own dangers to the heart.

Why this new edition?

Christian classics are extremely valuable but often hard to read. Unfamiliar vocabulary and sentence structure can obscure the original meaning. I hope that this modern adaptation makes Flavel's Biblical wisdom accessible to more readers.

Some of the changes in this modern translation include:

- New descriptive chapter and section headings.
- Modern English sentence structure and punctuation.
- Modern English vocabulary.
- Multiple sentences that break up long single sentences.
- New paragraph breaks for topic transitions.
- Sentence-level rewriting and rewording for clarity.
- ESV Scripture references.
- Footnotes with full verse quotations for ease of study.

The following passage provides an example of some of these changes:

Original passage:

"Pensive Soul, let this comfort thee, thy God designs thy benefit, even by these occasions of thy sad complaints; For (1.) Hereby he would let thee see what thy heart by Nature is and was, and therein take notice how much thou art beholding to free-Grace."

Revised passage:

"Pensive soul, let this comfort you: God is working for your good, even by these occasions of your sad complaints. For through these, He helps you to see what your heart is and was by nature and therein to appreciate how much you owe to free grace!"

The goal of this modern update is to capture the content and meaning of the original text as carefully as possible while improving the readability. I pray that this book encourages you to diligently keep your own heart for God's glory and your good!

Dedication

To my dearly beloved and longed-for flock of Jesus Christ in Dartmouth, over whom the Holy Spirit has made me an overseer. May you have sound judgment, true zeal, and unstained purity!

My dear friends, there are three sad sights where our eyes should continually affect our hearts. The first is to behold so many profane and degenerate individuals who bear the very image of Satan. Their outward conversation plainly discovers what they are and where they are going (Phil 3:18-19).[1] They look like themselves, the children of wrath.

It is also sad to see so many cursed hypocrites who, with astounding skill, artificially present themselves as saints so that even a judicious eye might sometimes mistake the work of the Spirit on them for His saving work on others. To hear such people confessing, praying, bemoaning their corruptions, and talking of their experiences, it is enough to be easily persuaded that they have the heart as well as the

---

[1] **Phil 3:18-19** "For many, of whom I have often told you and now tell you even with tears, walk as enemies of the cross of Christ. Their end is destruction, their god is their belly, and they glory in their shame, with minds set on earthly things."

face of a sincere Christian (for this is the way the people of God speak and pray and openly share their struggles). They look like saints, but they are not.

And it is sad to see so many real saints, in whom the Spirit of truth resides, face the impetuous workings of their corruptions but neglect to watch over their hearts. These individuals often fall into such scandalous practices that they look like hypocrites, but they are not.

These three sights are sad indeed, and oh that my head were waters and my eyes fountains of tears that I might weep abundantly over them all!

For the first, I would mourn heartily, considering that if they continue, they must be eternally damned (2 Thes 1:8-9;[2] 1 Cor 6:9[3]). For the second, I would both weep and tremble, considering that if they continue, they must be doubly damned (Matt 24:50-51).[4] And for the third, I would weep no less than any of the rest, because, though they themselves will be saved, yet their examples strengthen the bonds of death upon the other two (Matt 18:7).[5]

---

[2] **2 Thes 1:8-9** "In flaming fire, inflicting vengeance on those who do not know God and on those who do not obey the gospel of our Lord Jesus. They will suffer the punishment of eternal destruction, away from the presence of the Lord and from the glory of his might"

[3] **1 Cor 6:9** "Or do you not know that the unrighteous will not inherit the kingdom of God? Do not be deceived: neither the sexually immoral, nor idolaters, nor adulterers, nor men who practice homosexuality."

[4] **Matt 24:50-51** "The master of that servant will come on a day when he does not expect him and at an hour he does not know and will cut him in pieces and put him with the hypocrites. In that place there will be weeping and gnashing of teeth."

[5] **Mat 18:7** "Woe to the world for temptations to sin! For it is necessary that temptations come, but woe to the one by whom the temptation comes!"

Alas! That they should ever shed the blood of other souls, for whom Christ shed His own blood! That they should ever be cruel to others, who have experienced the kindness of Christ! I know they dare not do this directly and intentionally, but this is frequently the inevitable outcome. Permit me here to digress a little to contend with these prejudiced and hardened souls. Oh, why do you damage your own souls by the example of others? Because they stumble and break their shins, will you fall and break your necks? I wish that everyone who hardens themselves in this way and takes up a good opinion of their own deplorable condition would soberly consider and answer the following three questions.

1. Does our religion tolerate or support the sinful practices of its professors? Does it not rather impartially and severely condemn them? It is the glory of the Christian religion that it is pure and undefiled (James 1:27).[6] There is no doctrine so holy (Ps 19:8),[7] nor does any other make more provision for a holy life (Titus 2:11-12).[8] Indeed, there is a case where we may put the blame for the evil practices of others upon their principle, but that is when their practices naturally flow from and necessarily follows their principles. For example, if I see a Papist sin boldly, I may cry shame upon his principles that allow for the purchase of pardons, which creates a way for looseness. If I see

---

[6] **James 1:27** "Religion that is pure and undefiled before God the Father is this: to visit orphans and widows in their affliction, and to keep oneself unstained from the world."

[7] **Ps 19:8** "The precepts of the Lord are right, rejoicing the heart; the commandment of the Lord is pure, enlightening the eyes."

[8] **Titus 2:11-12** "For the grace of God has appeared, bringing salvation for all people, training us to renounce ungodliness and worldly passions, and to live self-controlled, upright, and godly lives in the present age."

an Arminian slight the grace of God while proudly advancing himself, I may cry shame upon his principles that directly lead to it. But can I accuse the underlying principles when others commit practices that are condemned and spoken against by the same principles that they avow?

2. Is it not most irrational to accuse religion because of the scandalous ways of some individuals, while simultaneously completely slighting and overlooking the holy and heavenly walk of many others? Are all who profess godliness loose and careless in their lives? No, some are an ornament to their faith and the glory of Christ. Why must the innocent be condemned with the guilty? Would you condemn the eleven disciples on the actions of one Judas?

3. Lastly, if you condemn Christianity because of the scandalous lives of some who profess to be Christians, must you not then cast off all religion in the world and become an atheist? Surely, this is the consequence of this thinking—for what religion is there where all who profess it walk according to its tenants? Consequently, you must, as Constantine told the Novatian, set up your ladder and get to heaven by yourself.

Alas! It is not our printed apologetics for Christianity, but the visible reformation of its followers that both saves its honor and removes the fatal stumbling blocks from unbelievers that causes them to stagger and fall into eternal punishment.

Now, there are two ways to accomplish this reformation. The first is to convince the consciences of believers of their sins, showing the evil and aggravation of them. The second is to address the heart to cleanse the fountain from which they proceed. For the first of these, a worthy and eminent servant of Christ has labored lately, holding a clear gospel glass before the faces of professing Christians to truly represent their spots and blemishes.[9] If the one who reads it will consider, apply, and practice it, this will doubtlessly lead to salvation. But if it has no good effect on the one who reads it, I know that it will become a testimony for him who wrote it. The second is the principal design of this small treatise, whose subject is exceedingly weighty and of daily use to the people of God. My treatment here may be attended with many defects and weaknesses; however, if it is not excellent, it may still be useful.

I will exercise your patience only long enough to tell you:

1. Why I published this treatise for the view of the world.
2. And why I direct it particularly to you.

First, as for the publication of this work, accept this sincere and brief account. In the same way that I was led to this subject by a special providence, I also was led to its publication by a kind of necessity. The providence that first led me to it was as follows. A dear and special friend of my intimate acquaintance, who was undergoing much inward turmoil due to a particular heart disorder, opened the case to me and earnestly requested some guidance and help in that regard. While I was bending my thoughts to that specific case, many other cases of similar importance (some of which depended on the first consideration) occurred to my thoughts. The scripture that I insist on here presented itself to me as a fit foundation for the whole discourse. After it was lengthened out to what you see now, several friends requested that I transcribe different parts of it for their use, as it addressed many different cases. Some others begged me to publish the whole work, which I was, in a sense, forced to do in order to save the pains of transcribing, which I find to be very tedious and tiresome work. And just as I had almost finished the copy, an opportunity presented itself (somewhat

---

[9] This likely refers to work by Lewis Stuckley, *A Gospel-Glass* (1667).

strangely) to make it public. So, from first to last, I have been carried beyond my first intentions in this work.

Some may say that the world is overflowing with books and, although the discourse is necessary, yet this publication is needless. To this, I answer that there are multitudes of books, indeed, but many of them do not concern themselves with root truths and practical godliness. Instead, they spend their strength on impractical notions and frivolous controversies, or they argue against foundational truths and endeavor to undermine the power of godliness. I could wish that those who have handled the pen of the scribe had done more with their time and effort than to thrust such useless discourses on the world. But there are some books that nourish the root and serve to clear, confirm, prepare, and apply the great truths of the Gospel so that they may be bread for souls to live and feed on. As for books in this category, I say that when farmers complain of too much corn, let Christians complain of too many such books.

And if you are so highly confident of your own knowledge and ability that such books are needless to you, let them alone, as they will do you no hurt. Other poor, hungry souls will be glad to have them and will bless God for what you despise and leave.

If you say that your condition is not addressed in the several cases handled here, I answer as follows. That which is not your condition may be another's condition. If you are placed in an easy, full, and prosperous state and, therefore, have no need of the help offered here to support your heart under pinching needs, others are forced to live by faith for every day's provision. If you are dawdled on the knee of providence, some of your brethren are under its feet. Maybe you have inward peace and tranquility of spirit and, therefore, do not need the counsel given here. But there are poor, afflicted souls who are ready to draw desperate conclusions about themselves in such times, and this may be a timely word for them. They may say as David said to Abigail,

"Blessed be the Lord, the God of Israel, who sent you" (1 Sam 25:39) and blessed be this book.

Furthermore, what is not your condition now may be your condition shortly. Do not say your mountain stands strong so that you will never be moved; there are changes in the right hand of the Most High. Then those truths which were little more esteemed than hedge-fruits will be like "apples of gold in a setting of silver" (Prov 25:11).[10] For this reason, Jeremiah taught the Jews (who at the time dwelt in their own land) how to defend their religion in Babylon and what they should say to the Chaldeans when they entered captivity (Jer 10:11).[11]

This concludes the reasons for this publication. As for the dedication of it to you, I was induced by the following considerations:

1. My relation to you is above all other people in the world. I look on my gifts as yours, my time as yours, and all the talents I am entrusted with as yours. It is not with you as a woman whose husband is dead and is then freed from the law of her husband; our relationship still continues along with all the mutual duties of it.

2. In consideration of my necessary absence from you, I would not want my absence to untwist the cord of friendship (as it typically does) by insensible degrees. Therefore, as absent friends often do, I have endeavored to preserve and strengthen our bond by this small remembrance. It was Vespasian's an-

---

[10] **Prov 25:11** "A word fitly spoken is like apples of gold in a setting of silver."

[11] **Jer 10:11** "Thus shall you say to them: 'The gods who did not make the heavens and the earth shall perish from the earth and from under the heavens.'" (Flavel states that this verse was written in the Chaldee language because it was to be used during their captivity in Babylon)

swer to Apollonius when he requested access for two philosophers: "My doors are always open to philosophers, but my very breast is open to you." I cannot say with him that my doors are open for the free access of friends, as my doors are, by a sad providence, shut against myself.[12] But this I can say, that my very breast is still open to you, and you are as dear to me as ever.

3. Another motivation for me (and indeed the main one) was the perpetual usefulness and necessity of these truths for you, which you will have continual need of. I know few of you have such good memories to retain these truths, and I cannot always be with you to teach these things. But *litera scripta manet* (the written word remains). I want to leave this with you as a legacy and a testimony of sincere love for and care over you. This may counsel and direct you when I cannot; I may be rendered useless to you by a civil or natural death, but this will out-live me. Oh, that it may serve your souls when I am silent in the dust!

To hasten now to a conclusion, I only have these three requests of you, which I earnestly beseech you not to deny me. Yes, I charge you, as ever you hope to appear with comfort before the great Shepherd, do not dare to slight these requests.

First, above all other studies in the world, study your own hearts! Do not waste a minute more of your precious time on frivolous and meaningless controversies; it is reported (how truly I do not know) that

---

[12] In 1662, the English Parliament passed the Act of Uniformity to enforce the beliefs and practices of the Church of England. Non-conforming protestants, like Flavel, were later prohibited from living near their former congregations. In this work, Flavel implies that he is a prisoner in his own home.

even Bellarmine turned with loathing from the academic study of divinity, because it lacked the sweet juice of piety. I would rather have it said of you, as one said of Swinkfeldius, that you lack a regular head but not an honest heart, rather than you have regular heads but irregular hearts. My dear flock, according to the grace given to me, I have labored in the course of my ministry among you to feed you with the heart-strengthening bread of practical doctrine. I assure you that it is far better for you to have the sweet, saving impressions of gospel-truths feelingly and powerfully conveyed to your hearts than to only understand them by reason alone or through dry logical inferences. Leave trifling studies to those who have time on their hands and do not know what to do with it.

Remember, you are at the door of eternity, and there is other work for you to do; those hours that you spend on heart-work in your closets are the golden spots of all your time and will have the sweetest influence on your last hour. Never forget those sermons I preached to you on that subject from 2 Kings 20:2-3.[13] Heart-work is weighty and difficult work, and an error here may cost you your souls. I may say of it as Augustine spoke of the doctrine of the Trinity: "a man can err in nothing more easily or more dangerously." Oh, then, study your hearts!

My next request is that you would carefully look at your speech and be truthful in all your ways. Hold forth the word of life, and make sure by the strictness and holiness of your lives to acquit yourselves in the very consciences of your enemies. Remember that your lives must culminate in that Great Day to judge the world (1 Cor 6:2).[14] Oh, then

---

[13] **2 Kings 20:2-3** "Then Hezekiah turned his face to the wall and prayed to the Lord, saying, 'Now, O Lord, please remember how I have walked before you in faithfulness and with a whole heart, and have done what is good in your sight.' And Hezekiah wept bitterly."

[14] **1 Cor 6:2** "Or do you not know that the saints will judge the world? And if the world is to be judged by you, are you incompetent to try trivial cases?"

what type of people ought you to be! You have many eyes watching you: the omniscient eyes of God that search hearts and minds (Rev 2:23),[15] the vigilant eyes of Satan (Job 1:7-8),[16] the envious eyes of enemies who carefully observe you (Ps 5:8),[17] and the quick and observant eyes of conscience, which none of your actions escape (Rom 9:1).[18]

Therefore, be clear and truthful in all your speech, and maintain the power of godliness in your private prayers and within your families. Then you will not fail to do so in your more public employments and interactions in the world. I have often told you that it is the honor of the Gospel that it makes the best parents and children, the best masters and servants, and the best husbands and wives in the world.

My third and last request is that you pray for me. I hope I can say (and I am sure that some of you have acknowledged) that I first came among you as the return of and answer to your prayers. And, indeed, it should be so (Luke 10:2).[19] I am also persuaded that I have been carried on in my work by your prayers, which is a sweet blessing (Eph

---

[15] **Rev 2:23** "And I will strike her children dead. And all the churches will know that I am he who searches mind and heart, and I will give to each of you according to your works."

[16] **Job 1:7-8** "The Lord said to Satan, 'From where have you come?' Satan answered the Lord and said, 'From going to and fro on the earth, and from walking up and down on it.' And the Lord said to Satan, 'Have you considered my servant Job, that there is none like him on the earth, a blameless and upright man, who fears God and turns away from evil?'"

[17] **Ps 5:8** "Lead me, O Lord, in your righteousness because of my enemies; make your way straight before me."

[18] **Rom 9:1** "I am speaking the truth in Christ—I am not lying; my conscience bears me witness in the Holy Spirit."

[19] **Luke 10:2** "And he said to them, 'The harvest is plentiful, but the laborers are few. Therefore pray earnestly to the Lord of the harvest to send out laborers into his harvest.'"

6:18-19).[20] And I hope by your prayers to receive an added benefit, even that which is mentioned in Hebrews 13:18-19[21] and Philemon 22.[22] And it truly is equal that you should pray for me, as I have often prayed for you. Let the pulpit, family, and prayer closet witness for me, and God forbid that I should sin against the Lord in ceasing to pray for you.

Yes, friends, your own interests may persuade you to it: what mercies you obtain for me rebound to your own advantage. If God preserves me, it is for your use and service. The more gifts and graces a minister has, the better for them that will follow his ministry; the more God fills me, the more I will be able to give out to you. I will detain you no longer, but I entreat you to accept this small testimony of my great love and to have access to it, according to the needs of your particular condition. Read it carefully and obediently. Judge it not by its elegance and style but by the weight and savor of what you read. It is a good rule of Bernard in *Legendis Libris* that in reading books, you should not so much regard the *science* as the *savor*. That this should prove to be the savor of life to you and to all those into whose hands it will come is the sincere desire of your loving and faithful pastor.

John Flavel
From my study at Ley in Slapton,
October 7, 1667

---

[20] **Eph 6:18-19** "Praying at all times in the Spirit, with all prayer and supplication. To that end, keep alert with all perseverance, making supplication for all the saints, and also for me, that words may be given to me in opening my mouth boldly to proclaim the mystery of the gospel."

[21] **Heb 13:18-19** "Pray for us, for we are sure that we have a clear conscience, desiring to act honorably in all things. I urge you the more earnestly to do this in order that I may be restored to you the sooner."

[22] **Philem 22** "At the same time, prepare a guest room for me, for I am hoping that through your prayers I will be graciously given to you."

Chapter 1

Keeping the Heart

"Keep your heart with all vigilance, for from it flow the springs of life." Proverbs 4:23

The heart of man is his worst part before regeneration and his best afterwards. It is the seat of principles and the fountain of actions. The eyes of God are principally fixed upon it and so should the eyes of the Christian.

The greatest difficulty in conversion is to win the heart to God, and the greatest difficulty after conversion is to keep the heart with God. Here we find the real center and emphasis of the Christian faith. Here is that which makes the way to life hard and the gate of heaven narrow (Matt 7:13-14).[1] The purpose of this book is to provide you with direction and help in this great work, which includes:

1. **An exhortation**: *Keep your heart with all vigilance!*
2. **The reason or motive for it**: *For from it flow the springs of life.*

---

[1] **Matt 7:13-14** "Enter by the narrow gate. For the gate is wide and the way is easy that leads to destruction, and those who enter by it are many. For the gate is narrow and the way is hard that leads to life, and those who find it are few."

The exhortation

In the exhortation to "keep your heart with all vigilance," I will consider the *matter of the duty* and the *manner of performing it*.

The matter of the duty is to *keep your heart*. The heart is not properly understood here as that noble member of the body that the philosophers call "the first that lives and the last that dies." Rather, in Scripture, the heart is sometimes used as a metaphor for some particular noble faculty of the soul. In Romans 1:21, it represents the understanding part when it says, "their foolish hearts," which is their understanding, "was darkened." And in Psalm 119:11, the heart is used to represent memory: "I have stored up your word in my heart." And in 1 John 3:20, it is used for the conscience, which places it in both the light of understanding and the recollection of the memory; when John says "our heart condemns us," he means our conscience, whose proper office it is to condemn.

But here we are to take it more generally for the whole soul, or inner being; for see how the heart relates to the body in the same way that the soul does to the person. And compare what health is to the heart in the way that holiness is to the soul: the state of the whole body depends on the soundness and vigor of the heart, and the everlasting state of the whole person depends on the good or ill condition of the soul.

Keeping the heart should be understood as the diligent and constant use and improvement of all holy means and duties to preserve the soul from sin and to maintain its sweet and free communion with God.[2]

---

[2] Flavel notes here: "I say *constant* because the reason added in the text extends the duty to all the states and conditions of a Christian's life, making it always binding. If the heart must be kept because out of it flow the issues of life, then as long as those issues of life flow out of it, we are obliged to keep it."

In regards to this text, Lavater[3] says the word is taken from a besieged garrison, which is not only attacked by many enemies from without but is in danger of being betrayed by the treacherous citizens within; in light of this danger, the soldiers, on pain of death, are commanded to watch.

And whereas the expression (keep your heart) seems to place this work upon us, it does not imply a sufficiency or ability in ourselves to do it. We are as able to stop the sun in its course or make the rivers run backward, as to rule and order our hearts by our own skill and power. We may as well be our own *saviors* than to be our own *keepers*. And yet Solomon speaks accurately enough when he says, "keep your heart," because though the duty is ours, the power is God's. A natural man has no power; a grace-filled man has some but not enough, and the power he does have depends on the animating and assisting strength of Christ. Grace within us is dependent on grace outside us:

> *"I am the vine; you are the branches. Whoever abides in me and I in him, he it is that bears much fruit, for apart from me you can do nothing." (John 15:5)*

The manner of performing this duty is *with all vigilance*. The Hebrew is very emphatic: *keeping with all keeping* (set double guards, or your heart will be lost). And the urgency of this expression used to bring us to this duty plainly implies how difficult it is to keep our hearts and how dangerous it is to let them go.

---

[3] Possibly referring to Ludwig Lavater, a Swiss Reformed theologian.

The motive

The reason or motive for this duty is very forcible and weighty: *"for from it flow the springs of life."* That is, it is the source and fountain of all vital actions and operations. Jerome says it is the spring and origin of both good and evil. like the spring in a watch that sets all the wheels in motion. The heart is the storehouse, whereas the hand and tongue are only storefronts; what is in the latter came from the former. The hand and tongue always begin where the heart ends. The heart plans and the members execute.

> *"The good person out of the good treasure of his heart produces good, and the evil person out of his evil treasure produces evil, for out of the abundance of the heart his mouth speaks." (Luke 6:45)*

So, then, if the heart errs in its work, these necessarily fail in theirs; for heart-errors are like errors at the start of a recipe, which cannot be corrected afterward; or they are like misplaced stamps and letters in the printing press which necessarily results in errors in all the printed copies. Oh, then! How important is the duty that is contained in the following proposition?

Doctrine:

> *Keeping and rightly managing the heart in every condition is the great business of a Christian's life.*

What the philosopher says of waters is as applicable to our hearts: it is hard to keep them within any bounds. God has set boundaries and limits to them, yet how frequently do they transgress them, not only the bounds of grace and faith but even of reason and common honesty. This is the reason why we labor with fear and trembling to our dying day. It is not the washing of hands that makes a Christian (for many hypocrites can show their hands to be just as clean); rather, it is the purifying, watching, and right ordering of the heart. This is the thing that provokes so many sad complaints and costs so many deep groans and tears. It was the pride of Hezekiah's heart that made him lie in the dust and mourn before the Lord (2 Chron 32:26).[4] It was the fear that hypocrisy might invade his heart that made David cry, "May my heart be blameless in your statutes, that I may not be put to shame" (Ps 119:80). It was the sad experience that he had of the divisions and distractions of his own heart in the service of God that made him pour out that prayer, "unite my heart to fear your name" (Ps 86:11).

The method that I will use to explore this doctrine is as follows:

1. First, I will look at the implications of keeping the heart and what it supposes.
2. Second, I will provide various reasons why we must make this the great work and business of our lives.
3. Third, I will point to different seasons that require special diligence in keeping the heart.
4. Finally, I will apply the whole teaching to several cases.

The implications of keeping the heart

Keeping the heart necessarily presupposes a prior work of sanctification, which has set the heart right by giving it a new spiritual bent and inclination. As long as the heart is *not set right* by grace with regard to its habitual frame, no duties or means can *keep it right* with God. The

---

[4] **2 Chron 32:26** "But Hezekiah humbled himself for the pride of his heart, both he and the inhabitants of Jerusalem, so that the wrath of the Lord did not come upon them in the days of Hezekiah."

self is the rudder of the unsanctified heart, which controls and moves it in all its designs and actions; and as long as this is so, it is impossible that any external means can keep it with God.

In creation, man possessed one constant frame and uniform tenor of Spirit, which held him to one straight and even course. Without one thought or faculty impaired or disordered, his mind was illuminated to perfectly understand, know, and comply with the will of God. His sensitive appetite and other inferior powers stood in a most obedient subordination to God.

However, man by degeneration has become a most disordered and rebellious creature, contesting with and opposing his Maker as the *first cause* by self-dependence, as the *ultimate good* by self-love, as the *highest Lord* by self-will, and as the *last end* by self-seeking. Consequently, he is quite disordered, and all his acts are irregular. Now, his illuminated understanding is clouded with ignorance, his compliant will is full of rebellion and stubbornness, and his subordinate powers cast off the dominion and government of superior faculties.

But by regeneration, the disordered soul is set right again; sanctification becomes the rectifying and due reframing, or as the Scripture phrases it, the renovation of the soul after the image of God (Eph 4:24).[5] Self-dependence is replaced by faith; self-love is replaced by the love of God; self-will gives way to subjection and obedience to the will of God; and self-seeking becomes self-denial. The darkened understanding is again illuminated (Eph 1:18),[6] the obstinate will is sweetly subdued

---

[5] **Eph 4:24** "And to put on the new self, created after the likeness of God in true righteousness and holiness."

[6] **Eph 1:18** "Having the eyes of your hearts enlightened, that you may know what is the hope to which he has called you, what are the riches of his glorious inheritance in the saints."

(Ps 110:3),[7] and the rebellious appetites and passions are gradually conquered (Rom 6:7).[8] And thus the soul, which sin had universally depraved, is again restored and rectified by grace.

This being presupposed, it is not difficult to understand what it is to keep the heart: it is nothing less than the constant care and diligence of this type of renewed man to preserve and daily maintain his soul in that holy frame that grace has placed him in.

For although grace has in great measure rectified the soul and given it a habitual and heavenly temperament, yet in practice sin often discomposes it again. In this way, even a gracious heart is like a musical instrument: no matter how perfectly it is tuned, a small matter brings it out of tune again before you can play another lesson on it. This is the case with gracious hearts; if they are engaged in one duty, yet how dull, dead, and disordered they are when they come to another. As a result, every duty needs a unique preparation of the heart:

> *"If you prepare your heart, you will stretch out your hands toward him." (Job 11:13)*

Therefore, to *keep the heart* is to carefully preserve it from sin, which disorders it, and to maintain that spiritual and gracious disposition that fits it for a life of communion with God. This includes the following six actions.

1. First, you must *frequently observe the frame of your heart*, looking within to examine its present condition. Carnal and proud individuals take no heed to this work, and they cannot be brought to confer

---

[7] **Ps 110:3** "Your people will offer themselves freely on the day of your power, in holy garments; from the womb of the morning, the dew of your youth will be yours."

[8] **Rom 6:7** "For one who has died has been set free from sin."

with their own hearts. There are some men and women who have lived forty or fifty years in the world and have scarce had one hour's discourse with their own hearts in all that time. It is a hard thing to bring an individual to this private meeting with the self on such an account. But saints know those soliloquies and self-conferences to have excellent uses and advantages. Even heathens acknowledge that the soul is made wise by sitting still in quietness. The penniless man does not care to look at his bank account, but an upright heart wants to know whether it goes up or down. "Let me meditate in my heart" (Ps 77:6).[9] You can never keep your hearts until you examine and understand its condition.

2. *Deeply humble yourself for heart evils and disorders.* This was Hezekiah's response when he humbled himself for the pride of his heart (2 Chron 32:26).[10] Similarly, the people were ordered to spread forth their hands to God in prayer in a sense of the affliction of their own hearts (1 Kings 8:38).[11] On this account, many upright hearts have been laid low before God, saying, *Oh what kind of heart do I have?* In their confessions, they point at the pained places of the heart: *Lord, here is the wound, here is the disease and sore.* A heart well-kept can be compared to the eye, which is a good metaphor for it: if a particle of dust gets into the eye, it will never stop winking and watering until it has wept it out; in the same way, the upright heart cannot rest until it has wept out its troubles and poured out its complaints before the Lord.

---

[9] **Ps 77:6** "I said, 'Let me remember my song in the night; let me meditate in my heart.' Then my spirit made a diligent search."

[10] **2 Chron 32:26** "But Hezekiah humbled himself for the pride of his heart, both he and the inhabitants of Jerusalem, so that the wrath of the Lord did not come upon them in the days of Hezekiah."

[11] **1 Kings 8:38** "Whatever prayer, whatever plea is made by any man or by all your people Israel, each knowing the affliction of his own heart and stretching out his hands toward this house."

3. When sin has defiled and disordered your heart, *offer earnest supplications and immediate prayers* for heart-purifying and sanctifying grace. "Declare me innocent from hidden faults" (Ps 19:12), and "unite my heart to fear your name" (Ps 86:11). Saints always have many of these petitions laid before the throne of grace; it is the thing that they most plead for from God. When they are praying for outward mercies, their spirits may happily be more remiss; but when it comes to heart-care, they exercise their spirits to the utmost, filling their mouths with pleas and cries for a better heart!

> *Oh, for a heart to love God more! To hate sin more! To walk more faithfully with God! Lord, do not deny me such a heart whatever else you deny me; Give me a heart to fear, love, and delight in You, even if I must beg for my bread in desolate places.*

It was observed of holy Mr. Bradford that when he was confessing sin, he would never cease confessing until he had felt some brokenness of heart for that sin, and when praying for any spiritual mercy, he would never stop until he had received some experience of that mercy. Thus, fervent prayer is the third action included in keeping the heart.

4. *Employ strong vows and bonds upon yourself* to walk more faithfully with God and to avoid the occasions that would cause your heart to sin. Well-composed, thoughtful, and deliberate vows can be of excellent use in some cases to guard the heart against some particular sin. "I have made a covenant with my eyes" (Job 31:1). In this way, holy ones have overawed their souls, preserving themselves from being defiled by some specific heart corruptions.

5. Maintain a *constant, holy jealousy for your own heart*; active self-jealousy is an excellent preservative from sin. If we will keep our hearts, we must have the eyes of our souls awake and open to all the disorderly and tumultuous stirrings of affections. If the affections break loose and the passions are stirred, the soul must discover and suppress them before they get to a height.

Oh, my soul, do you do well in this? My tumultuous thoughts and passions, from where do you come?

"Blessed is the one who fears the Lord always" (Prov 28:14). It is by this fear of the Lord that men depart from evil, shake off security, and preserve themselves from iniquity. Those who desire to keep the heart must partake with fear, rejoice with fear, and pass the whole time of their sojourning here in fear—all to keep the heart from sin.

6. Lastly, *sense God's presence with you and set the Lord always before you.* In this way, the people of God have found a singular means to keep their hearts upright and dissuade them from sin. When the eyes of our faith are fixed on the eyes of God's omniscience, we will not dare give license to our selfish thoughts and affections. What consideration moved holy Job to not permit his heart to yield to impure, vain thoughts? He tells us: "Does not he see my ways and number all my steps" (Job 31:4). Just as children in church would be playing with their toys if their parents were not seated behind them, so also would the hearts of the best saints if it were not for the eyes of God.

In these and similar practices, gracious souls demonstrate the care that they have for their hearts. They are as careful to prevent their corruptions from breaking loose in a time of temptation as seamen are to bind their canons securely to the ship during a storm. They are as careful to preserve the sweetness and comfort that they receive from God in any duty as one who comes out of a hot bath is to preserve the warmth when going out into the chill air. This is our work, and of all the works of our faith, it is the most difficult, constant, and important work.

Heart-work is the *hardest work* indeed. It takes no great effort to shuffle through religious duties with a loose and careless spirit; but to tie up your loose and vain thoughts, to set yourself before the Lord in a constant and serious attendance upon Him, this will cost you something. It is easy to attain a familiarity and ability in the language of prayer, putting your meaning into apt and appropriate expressions; but to get your heart broken for sin while you are confessing it, to be melted with free grace while you are blessing God for it, to be really humbled and ashamed when contemplating God's infinite holiness, and to keep your heart in this frame—not only in but after this duty—will surely cost you some groans and painful exertions in your soul. It is no great matter to repress the outward acts of sin and to compose the external part of your life in an attractive and acceptable manner (even carnal persons can achieve this by the force of common principles); but to kill the root of corruption within, to set and keep up a holy government over your thoughts, and to lay all things straight and orderly in the heart, this is not easy.

Heart-work is *constant work*. The keeping of the heart is never done until life is done; our labor and this life ends together. For Christians, this work is like that of seamen who have sprung a leak at sea—if they do not constantly work the pumps, the water rises and will quickly sink them. It is pointless for them to say the work is hard or that they are weary. There is no time or condition in the life of a Christian that will allow for an intermission of this work. The work of keeping watch over our hearts is like the keeping up of Moses's hands while Israel and Amalek were fighting below; the minute the hands of Moses grew heavy

29

and sunk down, Amalek began to prevail (Ex 17:12).[12] You know it cost David and Peter many sad days and nights for neglecting to watch over their own hearts for only a few minutes.

Heart-work is the *most important work* of a Christian's life. Without this, we are only formalists in religion, and all our professions, gifts, and duties signify nothing.

"My son, give me your heart." (Prov 23:26)

God is pleased to call the heart a gift, which is in fact a debt. He puts the honor on you to receive your heart from you as a gift, but if this is not given to Him, He disregards whatever else you bring. The worth or value in what we do is directly related to the heart we put into it. Concerning the heart, God seems to say what Joseph said of Benjamin, "You shall not see my face unless your brother is with you" (Gen 43:3). Among the heathens, when an animal was cut up for sacrifice, the first thing the priest looked at was the heart; if that was unsound and unacceptable, the sacrifice was rejected. In the same way, God rejects all duties—no matter how glorious in other respects—that are offered to Him without a heart. The one who heedlessly performs a duty without a heart is no more accepted with God than the one who performs it with a duplicitous heart (Isa 66:3).[13]

---

[12] **Ex 17:12** "But Moses' hands grew weary, so they took a stone and put it under him, and he sat on it, while Aaron and Hur held up his hands, one on one side, and the other on the other side. So his hands were steady until the going down of the sun."

[13] **Isa 66:3** "He who slaughters an ox is like one who kills a man; he who sacrifices a lamb, like one who breaks a dog's neck; he who presents a grain offering, like one who offers pig's blood; he who makes a memorial offering of frankincense, like one who blesses an idol. These have chosen their own ways, and their soul delights in their abominations."

Thus, I have briefly opened the nature of the duty to show what is meant by the phrase, "*Keep your heart.*"

Chapter 2

Why Keep the Heart?

I will next proceed to give some reasons why we should make keeping the heart the great business of our lives. The importance and necessity of making this our primary aim will manifestly appear in the following ways:

1. The glory of God.
2. The sincerity of our profession.
3. The beauty of our conversation.
4. The comfort of our souls.
5. The improvement of our graces.
6. The ability to withstand temptation.

These are all wrapped up in and dependent on our sincerity and care in the management of this heart-work.

The glory of God

The glory that we give to God is dependent on this duty; for heart-evils are very provoking evils to the Lord. Theologians have done well to observe that outward sins are *majoris infamiae*, sins of greater infamy, but heart-sins are *majoris reatus*, sins of deeper guilt. How severely has our great God declared His wrath from heaven against heart-wickedness? The great crime for which the old world stood indicted was heart-wickedness:

> *"The Lord saw that the wickedness of man was great in the earth, and that every intention of the thoughts of his heart was only evil continually." (Gen 6:5)*

For this reason, he sent the most dreadful judgment that was ever executed since the world began:

> *"So the Lord said, 'I will blot out man whom I have created from the face of the land, man and animals and creeping things and birds of the heavens, for I am sorry that I have made them.'" (v. 7)*

We do not find their murders, adulteries, and blasphemies particularly alleged against them (though they were defiled with these sins); rather, God calls out the evil of their hearts. And it was this heart-evil that so provoked God that He gave up His special inheritance into the hands of their enemies:

> *"O Jerusalem, wash your heart from evil, that you may be saved. How long shall your wicked thoughts lodge within you?" (Jer 4:14)*

God took special notice of the wickedness and vanity of their thoughts; consequently, the Chaldean must come upon them as a "lion… from his thicket" (v. 7) and tear them to pieces. God also threw down the fallen angels of heaven for the same thought-sins, and He keeps them still in everlasting chains for the judgment of the Last Day, by which expression is clearly implying some extraordinary judgment that is reserved for them—like prisoners who, having the most chains, are supposed to be the greatest criminal offenders. And what was their sin? It was only spiritual wickedness, for they had no physical bodies to act out externally against God.

In fact, mere heart-evils are so provoking that because of them, He rejects with indignation all the duties that some men perform for Him:

"He who slaughters an ox is like one who kills a man; he who sacrifices a lamb, like one who breaks a dog's neck; he who presents a grain offering, like one who offers pig's blood; he who makes a memorial offering of frankincense, like one who blesses an idol."
(Isa 66:3)

In what words could abhorrence of a creature's actions be more fully expressed by the holy God? Murder and idolatry are not more repulsive in His account than their sacrifices, though their practice was appointed by Him. What made them so vile? The following words tell us: "Their soul delights in their abominations" (v. 3).

To conclude, such is the vileness of mere heart-sins that Scripture sometimes suggests a difficulty in their pardon. This was the case of Simon the magician (Acts 8:21);[1] his heart was not right because he had vile thoughts of God and the things of God. The Apostle tells him to "Repent, therefore, of this wickedness of yours, and pray to the Lord that, if possible, the intent of your heart may be forgiven you" (Acts 8:22). Oh, then, never underestimate heart-evils! For by these God is highly wronged and provoked. Therefore, let all of us make it our work to keep our hearts with all diligence!

---

[1] **Acts 8:21** "You have neither part nor lot in this matter, for your heart is not right before God."

The sincerity of our profession

The sincerity of our profession of faith depends greatly on the care and conscience that we have in keeping our hearts. No matter how proficient a man is in the externals of religion, he is most certainly a hypocrite if he is heedless and careless of the frame of his own heart. We see an instance of this in the case of Jehu:

"Jehu was not careful to walk in the law of the Lord, the God of Israel, with all his heart." (2 Kings 10:31)

The earlier account described the great service that Jehu performed against the house of Ahab and Baal, as well as the great temporal reward that God gave him for that service—namely, that his children to the fourth generation would sit on the throne of Israel. Yet in these words, Jehu is reprimanded for being a hypocrite; although God approved and rewarded the work, yet He abhorred and rejected the person that did it hypocritically. And where did his hypocrisy lie? In this, that he took no heed to walk in the ways of the Lord with his heart; he did everything insincerely and for selfish ends. Although the work he did was materially good, yet by not purging his heart from unworthy and selfish designs in doing it, he became a hypocrite. And though Simon the magician, whom we spoke of before, presented himself well so that the Apostle could not immediately censure him, yet his hypocrisy was quickly discovered. But how? Though he professed and associated himself with the saints, yet he was a stranger to the mortification of heart-sins: "your heart is not right before God" (Acts 8:21).

It is true that there is a great difference among Christians themselves in their diligence and aptitude for heart-work. Some are more familiar and successful in it than others, but the man who takes no heed to his heart and fails to carefully order it rightly before God is only a hypocrite:

"And they come to you as people come, and they sit before you as my people, and they hear what you say but they will not do it; for with lustful talk in their mouths they act; their heart is set on their gain." (Ezek 33:31)

This verse describes a group of formal hypocrites, which is evident by the expression, *"as my people,"* which implies they are *like* them but not *of* them. And what made them so? Their outside was attractive with reverent postures, lofty professions of faith, and seemingly much joy and delight in ordinances; "you are to them like one who sings" (v. 32). But for all that, they did not keep their hearts with God in those duties. Their hearts were controlled by their lusts, and they went after their gain. Had they kept their hearts with God, all would be well; but by not regarding which way their heart went in duty, they laid the foundation for their hypocrisy.

Of course, you might object that if any upright soul should reach this conclusion, then you must be a hypocrite too, for many times your heart departs from God in duty. Do what you will, yet you cannot hold it solely with God.

To this, I answer, the very objection carries in it its own solution. You say, "do what I can, yet I cannot keep my heart with God." Soul, if you do what you can, you have the blessing of an upright heart, though God may see it good to exercise you under the affliction of a discomposed heart. There remains still some wildness in the thoughts and imaginations of the best men and women to humble them; but if you find a care to prevent them ahead of time and to oppose them when they appear, along with grief and sorrow afterward, you will find enough to clear you from reigning hypocrisy. This preparation is seen partly in laying up the word in your heart to prevent them:

"I have stored up your word in my heart, that I might not sin against you." (Ps 119:11)

Our sincerity is seen partly in our endeavors to engage our hearts toward God and partly in pleading for protecting grace from God in the outset of our duties (Ps 119:36-37).[2] It is a good sign when care goes before duty. It is also a sweet sign of uprightness to oppose these thoughts in their first appearance:

"I hate the double-minded, but I love your law." (Ps 119:113)

"The desires of the Spirit are against the flesh." (Gal 5:17)

Lastly, your grief afterward discovers your upright heart. If with Hezekiah you are humbled for the evils of your heart, you have no reason from these disorders to question the integrity of it. But to allow sin to lodge quietly in the heart and to let your heart habitually and unrestrainedly wander from God, this is a sad and dangerous symptom indeed!

The beauty of our conversation

The beauty of our conversation arises from the heavenly frames and holy order of our spirits; there is a spiritual luster and beauty in the conversation of saints:

"One who is righteous is a guide to his neighbor." (Prov 12:26)

---

[2] Ps 119:36-37 "Incline my heart to your testimonies, and not to selfish gain! Turn my eyes from looking at worthless things; and give me life in your ways."

They shine as the lights of the world; the luster and beauty of their lives comes from the excellency of their spirits, like a candle within that puts a luster on the lantern in which it shines. It is impossible that a disordered and neglected heart should ever produce a well-ordered conversation; and since (as the text observes) the issues or streams of life flow out of the fountain of the heart, it must necessarily follow that as the heart is, so the life will be. "Abstain from the passions of the flesh…keep your conduct among the Gentiles honorable" (1 Pet 2:11-12),[3] or beautiful as the word implies in the Greek.

> "Let the wicked forsake his way, and the unrighteous man his thoughts." (Isa 55:7)

His *way* notes the course of his life, and his *thoughts* reveal the frame of his heart. And, therefore, since the way and course of his life flows from his thoughts, or the frame of his heart, both or neither will be forsaken. The heart is the womb of all actions, for these actions are virtually and seminally contained in our thoughts, and after these thoughts are made up into affections, they quickly materialize into suitable actions and practices. If the heart is wicked, then as Christ says:

> "Out of the heart come evil thoughts, murder, adultery, sexual immorality, theft, false witness, slander." (Matt 15:19)

Note the order: first evil and vengeful thoughts, and then unclean and murderous practices.

---

[3] **1 Pet 2:11-12** "Beloved, I urge you as sojourners and exiles to abstain from the passions of the flesh, which wage war against your soul. Keep your conduct among the Gentiles honorable, so that when they speak against you as evildoers, they may see your good deeds and glorify God on the day of visitation."

And if the heart is holy and spiritual, then, as David says from sweet experience:

"My heart overflows with a pleasing theme; I address my verses to the king; my tongue is like the pen of a ready scribe." (Ps 45:1)

Here is a life that is richly beautified with good works, some already made ("I address my verses") and others in the process of making ("My heart overflows") but both proceeding from the heavenly frame of his heart.

Only put the heart in frame, and the life will quickly follow. It is not difficult, I think, to discern the frame of a Christian's heart by observing their duties and conversations. Take a man in a good frame, and see how serious, heavenly, and profitable are his conversations and duties! What a lovely companion he is in this state! It would do anyone's heart good to be with him at such a time:

"The mouth of the righteous utters wisdom, and his tongue speaks justice. The law of his God is in his heart; his steps do not slip."
(Ps 37:30-31)

When the heart is close to God and full of God, how skillfully and intelligently he engages in spiritual discourse, improving every occasion and advantage for some heavenly purpose. Few words are wasted.

And what else can be the reason why the discourses and duties of many Christians have become so trivial and unprofitable? Why has their communion with both God and one another become like a dry stalk? It is only because their hearts are neglected. Surely, this must be the reason for it, and it is truly an evil that is greatly to be mourned; for because of this, Christian fellowship has become a lifeless thing so that the attracting beauty, which was meant to shine from the conversations of the saints upon the faces and consciences of the world, is for the most part lost (even if this does not attract unbelievers and bring them to love God, yet at least it leaves a testimony in their consciences of the excellency of believers and their ways). This is to the unspeakable detriment of our Faith.

There was a time when Christians did display this attractiveness to such an extent that the world stood in awe of them (1 Pet 4:4).[4] Their life and language were of such a different strain from others, while their tongues revealed them to be Galileans wherever they went. But today, many professors of Christianity have engaged in vain speculations and fruitless controversies, while also neglecting heart-work and practical godliness. Consequently, the case is sadly altered: their discourse has become like other men. If they come among you now, they may, to borrow a phrase, hear each one "speak in his own language" (Acts 2:6). And, truly, I have little hope to see this evil corrected and the credit of the Christian religion repaired until Christians again resume their old work—that is, until they attend closer to heart-work. When the salt of heavenly-mindedness is again cast into the spring, the streams will run clearer and sweeter.

The comfort of our souls

The comfort of our souls depends greatly on the keeping of our hearts; for those who are negligent in attending to their hearts are usually utter strangers to the assurance and sweet comforts that flow from it.

---

[4] **1 Pet 4:4** "With respect to this they are surprised when you do not join them in the same flood of debauchery, and they malign you."

Indeed, if the Antinomian[5] doctrine were true, which teaches you to reject any marks or signs that point to your current spiritual condition, then you might be careless of your hearts, or even strangers to them, and yet have comfort. They believe that it is only the Spirit that immediately assures you of your salvation by witnessing your adoption directly apart from any self-examination. However, since both Scripture and experience refute this false teaching, I hope you will never look for comfort in that unbiblical way. I do not deny that it is the work and office of the Spirit to assure you, but I strongly believe that if you are ever to attain assurance in the typical way that God dispenses it, you must labor with your own hearts. You may expect your comforts on easier terms, but I am mistaken if you ever enjoy them on any other. The pattern in Scripture is to "be all the more diligent" (2 Pet 1:10)[6] and to "examine yourselves" (2 Cor 13:5).[7]

I remember Mr. Roberts, in his treatise on the covenant, who recounted a newly converted Christian who so vehemently panted after the infallible assurance of God's love, that for a long time he earnestly desired some voice from heaven; he even sometimes walked alone through the fields, earnestly desiring some miraculous voice from the trees and stones he passed. After much desire and longing, he was denied this request. However, in time, a better assurance was provided in the ordinary way of searching the Word and his own heart. Gerson recounts a similar experience of one who was driven by temptation to the

---

[5] Antinomianism is a belief that Christians, being freed by grace, are also freed from any adherence to the moral law.

[6] **2 Pet 1:10** "Therefore, brothers, be all the more diligent to confirm your calling and election, for if you practice these qualities you will never fall."

[7] **2 Cor 13:5** "Examine yourselves, to see whether you are in the faith. Test yourselves. Or do you not realize this about yourselves, that Jesus Christ is in you?— unless indeed you fail to meet the test!"

very edge of desperation before, at last, being sweetly settled and assured. When asked how he attained it, he answered that it was not by any extraordinary revelation but by subjecting his understanding to the Scriptures and by comparing his own heart with them.

The Spirit indeed assures by witnessing to our adoption, and He does this in two ways. First, objectively, the Spirit manifests those graces in our souls that are the conditions of the promise, and, therefore, the Spirit and His graces in us are all one. The Spirit of God dwelling in us is a mark of our adoption. Now, the Spirit cannot be discerned in His essence but in His operations; to discern these is to discern the Spirit. And I cannot imagine how these can be discerned without serious searching and diligent watching of the heart. The second way the Spirit witnesses to our adoption is effectively by illuminating the soul with a grace-discovering light that shines upon His own work. In the natural order, this follows the former work. He first infuses grace and then opens the eye of the soul to see it. Now, since the heart is the subject of that infused grace, even this way of the Spirit's witnessing also includes the necessity to carefully keep our own hearts.

A neglected heart is so confused and dark that the little grace which is in it is not ordinarily discernable. The most conscientious and diligent Christians, who make the most effort and spend the most time with their hearts, still find it very difficult to discover the pure and genuine workings of the Spirit in them. How, then, will the negligent Christian, who is comparatively remiss about heart-work, ever be able to discover it? Sincerity, which is the thing we fight for, lies in the heart like a small piece of gold in the bottom of a river; he who wishes to find it must stay until the water is clear and settled, and then he will see it sparkling at the bottom. And for our hearts to be clear and settled, how much effort, careful watching, and diligence will it cost us?

God does not usually indulge lazy and negligent souls with the comforts of assurance, for He does not patronize sloth and carelessness. God gives assurance, but it will be in His own way. His command has united our care and comfort together, and it is a mistake to think that the beautiful child of assurance may be born without pangs. Ah, how many solitary hours have the people of God spent in heart-examination? How many times have they looked into the Word and then into their hearts? Sometimes, they thought they discovered sincerity and were even ready to come to the triumphant conclusion of assurance. But then a doubt appears that they cannot resolve, and they find their hopes dashed. Many hopes, fears, doubts, and reasonings are breathed out before they arrive at a peaceful assurance.

To conclude, even if it were possible for a careless Christian to attain assurance, yet it would be impossible that he would long retain it. One whose heart is enlarged with the joys of assurance is like a pregnant woman who is prone to miscarriages: if extraordinary care is not taken, it is a thousand to one if she ever embraces a living child. In the same way, a little pride, vanity, or carelessness dashes all that you have been laboring for so long in many weary duties. Therefore, since the joy of your life and the comfort of your soul rises and falls without diligence in this work, keep your heart with all diligence!

The improvement of our graces

The improvement of our graces depends on the keeping of our hearts; I never knew grace to thrive in a negligent and careless soul. The habits and roots of grace are planted in the heart, and the deeper they are established there, the more thriving and flourishing grace is. In Ephesians, we read of being rooted in grace (Eph 3:17).[8] Grace in the heart is the root of every gracious word in the mouth and every holy

---

[8] **Eph 3:17** "So that Christ may dwell in your hearts through faith—that you, being rooted and grounded in love."

43

work in the hand (2 Cor 4:13).[9] It is true that Christ is the root of a Christian, but Christ is the originating root, and grace is the root originated, planted, and influenced by Christ. And the acts of grace are fruitful and vigorous to the extent that they thrive under divine influences. Now, when a heart is not kept with care and diligence, these fruitful influences are stopped and cut off, and multitudes of vanities break in upon it and devour its strength. The heart is, so to speak, a pasture in which multitudes of thoughts are fed every day. A gracious heart, which is diligently kept, feeds many precious thoughts of God in a day:

"How precious to me are your thoughts, O God!
How vast is the sum of them!
If I would count them, they are more than the sand.
I awake, and I am still with you." (Ps 139:17-18)

And as the gracious heart feeds and nourishes them, they refresh and satisfy the heart:

"My soul will be satisfied as with fat and rich food,
and my mouth will praise you with joyful lips,
when I remember you upon my bed,
and meditate on you in the watches of the night." (Ps 63:5-6)

But in the untended heart, swarms of vain and foolish thoughts are perpetually working, pushing out those spiritual ideas and thoughts of God that could refresh the soul.

---

[9] **2 Cor 4:13** "Since we have the same spirit of faith according to what has been written, 'I believed, and so I spoke,' we also believe, and so we also speak."

Besides, the careless heart makes little of any duty or ordinance it performs or attends to, and yet these are the conduits of heaven from which grace is watered and made fruitful. You may go with a heedless spirit from ordinance to ordinance, abide in all your duties under the finest teaching, and yet never be improved by them; for heart-neglect is a leak in the bottom, and no heavenly influences—no matter how rich—abide in such a soul (Matt 13:4).[10] This type of heart lies open and common like the highway that is free for all travelers, so when the seed falls on it, the birds come to devour it. Alas! It is not enough to hear, unless you take heed *how* you hear. You may pray and never be any better for it unless you attend to your prayers. In a word, all ordinances, means, and duties are blessed for the improvement of grace in us in proportion to the care and strictness we use in keeping our hearts in them.

The ability to withstand temptation

Lastly, the stability of our souls in the hour of temptation depends greatly on the care and conscience we have in the keeping of our hearts. The careless heart is an easy prey for Satan in the hour of temptation, and his main cannons are raised against that fort-royal, the heart. If he wins the heart, he wins all, for it commands the whole man. And, alas, how easy a conquest is a neglected heart? It is no more difficult to surprise it than for an enemy to enter a city whose gates are open and unguarded. However, the watchful heart discovers and suppresses the temptation before it comes to its strength. Theologians observe this to be the method in which temptations are ripened and brought to their full strength:

---

[10] **Matt 13:4** "And as he sowed, some seeds fell along the path, and the birds came and devoured them."

1. There is the irritation of an object or the power that it has to work upon and provoke our corrupt nature, which is either done by the actual presence of the object or by imagination, when the object (though absent) is held out before the soul.

2. Then there is the motion of the sensitive appetite, which is stirred and provoked by the desire, representing it as a sensual good for profit or pleasure.

3. A consultation follows in the mind, deliberating about the likeliest means of accomplishing it.

4. Next, there is a decision or choice of the will.

5. And, lastly, the will is fully engaged to achieve its desire.

All this may happen in a few moments, for the debates of the soul are quick and soon ended; when it comes this far, then the heart is won; Satan has entered victoriously and displayed his colors on the wall of that royal fort. But had the heart been well-guarded at first, it would never have come to this height; the temptation would have been stopped in the first or second act. Indeed, it is easily stopped there, for the motions of a tempted soul to sin is like the motion of a stone falling from the brow of a hill: it is easily stopped at first, but once it starts rolling, it is hard to stop. Therefore, it is the greatest wisdom in the world to observe the first motions of the heart, to check and stop sin there. The motions of sin are weakest at first, so a little care and watchfulness at the outset may prevent much mischief that would otherwise bring the careless heart under the power of temptation, like the Syrians when they were brought blindfolded into the midst of Samaria before they knew where they were.

At this point, reader, I hope you are fully satisfied with how consequential and necessary a work it is to keep your heart. So many interests of the soul are bound up in this duty.

Chapter 3

A Season of Prosperity

Now, according to the proposed method, I will proceed to point out those special seasons in the life of a Christian that require and call for the utmost diligence in keeping the heart. For although—as we previously observed—we are continually bound to this duty and there is no time or condition of life in which we may be excused from this work, yet there are some unique seasons, critical moments, which require more than a common vigilance over the heart.

And the first season is a time of prosperity when providence smiles on us and dangles us upon her knee. At this moment, Christian, keep your heart with all diligence! For it will be exceedingly apt to grow secure, proud, and earthly. As Bernard said, to see a man humble in prosperity is one of the greatest rarities in the world. Even a good Hezekiah could not hide a self-exalting temperament under this temptation. And it is the reason for the caution to Israel:

> "And when the Lord your God brings you into the land that he swore to your fathers, to Abraham, to Isaac, and to Jacob, to give you—with great and good cities that you did not build, and houses full of all good things that you did not fill, and cisterns that you did not dig, and vineyards and olive trees that you did not plant—and

when you eat and are full, then take care lest you forget the Lord, who brought you out of the land of Egypt, out of the house of slavery." (Deut 6:10-12)

And, indeed, so it happened; for "Jeshurun grew fat, and kicked" (Deut 32:15).[1] This raises a question: *how can we keep our hearts from pride and carnal security under the smiles of providence and access to earthly comforts?* There are seven excellent considerations to help secure the heart from the dangerous snares of prosperity.

How hard it is for the rich to be saved

Consider the dangerous and ensnaring temptations that attend a pleasant and prosperous condition. In fact, very few of those that live in the pleasures and prosperity of this world escape everlasting punishment. Consider the words of Jesus:

"Again I tell you, it is easier for a camel to go through the eye of a needle than for a rich person to enter the kingdom of God." (Matt 19:24)

And Paul noted that among the Corinthian Christians, "not many were powerful, not many were of noble birth" (1 Cor 1:26).

We would be right to tremble when Scripture tells us that, in general, few will be saved; how much more should we tremble when we learn that among those of our rank and class, it is even less. When Joshua called all the tribes of Israel to be chosen by lot to discover the sin of Achan, doubtless Achan feared; when the tribe of Judah was

---

[1] **Deut 32:15** "But Jeshurun grew fat, and kicked; you grew fat, stout, and seek; then he forsook God who made him and scoffed at the Rock of his salvation."

taken, his fear increased; but when the family of the Zerahites was taken, it was then time to tremble.[2] Similarly, when Scripture comes so near as to tell us that of the prosperous very few will escape, it is time to look around. "I should wonder," says Chrysostom, "if any of the rulers are saved."

Oh, how many have been chauffeured to hell in the carriages of earthly pleasures, while others have been whipped to heaven by the rod of affliction? How few, like the daughter of Tyre, come to Christ with a gift (Ps 45:12)![3] How few among the rich entreat His favor?

Experience of past believers

It may keep us yet more humble and watchful in prosperity if we consider how many Christians have been the worse for it. How much better would it have been for some of them if they had never known prosperity? When they were in a low condition, how humble, spiritual, and heavenly they were; but when they became prosperous, there was a visible alteration of their spirits. This was the experience of Israel; when they were in a low condition in the wilderness, then Israel was "holy to the Lord" (Jer 2:2-3).[4] But when they came into Canaan and were fed in a fat pasture, then they said, "we are free, we will come no more to you" (v. 31).

Outward gains are ordinarily accompanied by inward losses. In a low condition, our daily lives are likely to take on the aroma of our duties; but in an exalted condition, our duties often take on the aroma of

[2] See Joshua 7.

[3] **Ps 45:12** "And the daughter of Tyre shall be there with a gift; even the rich among the people shall intreat thy favour." (KJV)

[4] **Jer 2:2-3** "I remember the devotion of your youth, your love as a bride, how you followed me in the wilderness, in a land not sown. Israel was holy to the Lord, the firstfruits of his harvest."

the world. He is indeed rich in grace whose graces are not hindered by his riches. There are very few Jehoshaphats in the world, of whom it was said, "he had great riches and honor" and "his heart was courageous in the ways of the Lord" (2 Chron 17:5-6). Will this not keep your heart humble in prosperity to think how many godly people have paid dearly for their riches, losing that which all the world cannot purchase?

God's judgment

Keep down your vain heart by this consideration that *God values no one a bit more for these things*. God values no one by outward achievements but by inward graces, which are the internal ornaments of the Spirit and of great worth in God's eyes (1 Pet 3:4).[5] He despises all worldly glory and shows no partiality, "but in every nation anyone who fears him and does what is right is acceptable to him" (Acts 10:35). Indeed, if the judgment of God followed the same rule that the world uses, we might value ourselves by these things and stand upon them; but as one said when dying, "I will not appear before God as a doctor but as a man." All of us are no more than what God judges us to be. Does your heart still swell, and will neither of the former considerations keep it humble?

Lifelong regrets

Next, consider how bitterly many people at the approach of death have mourned their folly that they ever set their hearts on material possessions and heartily wished that they had never known them. What a

---

[5] **1 Pet 3:4** "But let your adorning be the hidden person of the heart with the imperishable beauty of a gentle and quiet spirit, which in God's sight is very precious."

sad story was that of Pius Quintus, who as he was dying cried out despairingly, "When I was in a low condition, I had some hopes of salvation, but when I was advanced to be a cardinal, I greatly doubted it, but since I became pope, I have no hope at all." Mr. Spencer also tells us a true but sad story of a rich oppressor who had accumulated a great estate for his only son; when he came to die, he called his son to him and said, "Son, do you indeed love me?" The son answered that both nature and his paternal indulgence obliged him to say yes; then the Father said, "Express it by this: hold your finger in the candle as long as I am saying the Lord's Prayer." The son attempted it but could not endure it; whereupon the Father broke out into these expressions: "You cannot suffer the burning of your finger for me, but to get this wealth, I have hazarded my soul for you and must burn body and soul in hell for your sake. Your pains would have been but for a moment, but mine will be unquenchable fire."

Distractions of prosperity

We can keep our hearts humble by considering how obstructing earthly things are to our souls being heartily engaged in the way to heaven. These things can shut out much of heaven from us in the present even if they do not shut us out of heaven in the end. If you consider yourself to be a stranger in this world who is traveling toward heaven to find a better country, then you have no more reason to be captivated and delighted by earthly things than a weary horse has with a heavy saddlebag. There was a serious truth in that atheistic scoff of Julian when he took away the Christians' estates and told them it was to make them fitter for the Kingdom of Heaven.

Greater responsibilities

Knowing all this, is your spirit still proud and lofty? Then urge yourself to consider that awful day of reckoning, where we will be asked to give an account for all the mercies shown to us. And I think this should awe and humble the proudest heart that ever resided in the breast of a saint. Know for certain that the Lord records all the mercies that He ever gave to you, from the beginning of your life to the end (Mic 6:5).[6] Yes, they are exactly numbered and recorded for the purposes of accounting, and your account will be commensurate.

> *"Everyone to whom much was given, of him much will be required."*
> (Luke 12:48)

You are only stewards, and your Lord will come to take an account of you. Therefore, for you who have so much of this world in your hands, how great an account must you make? What witnesses will your enemies be against you on that day if you have made no better use of your earthly resources?

The call to humility

It is very humbling to think that the mercies of God should work differently on my spirit than they did on the spirits of past saints, to whom they came as sanctified mercies from the love of God. Ah, Lord! What a sad consideration is this? It is enough to lay me in the dust when I consider the following examples.

---

[6] **Mic 6:5** "O my people, remember what Balak king of Moab devised, and what Balaam the son of Beor answered him, and what happened from Shittim to Gilgal, that you may know the righteous acts of the Lord."

Consider that God's mercies have greatly humbled past saints. The higher that God raised them, the lower they laid themselves before God. For example, after God had given Jacob great possession (Gen 32:5),[7] Jacob said:

"I am not worthy of the least of all the deeds of steadfast love and all the faithfulness that you have shown to your servant, for with only my staff I crossed this Jordan, and now I have become two camps." (Gen 32:10)

And it was the same way with holy David. When God confirmed the promise to him, to build him a house and not to reject him as he did Saul, David went in before the Lord and said:

"Who am I, O Lord God, and what is my house, that you have brought me thus far?" (2 Sam 7:18)

And when Israel was to bring God the first fruits of Canaan, God required them to say, "A wandering Aramean was my father" (Deut 26:5).[8] Do others raise God higher for raising them? And the more God raises me, shall I abuse Him and exalt myself? Oh, what a sad thing this is!

Others have freely ascribed the glory of all their enjoyments to God and magnified not themselves, but Him, for their mercies. This was true of David when he said:

---

[7] **Gen 32:5** "I have oxen, donkeys, flocks, male servants, and female servants."

[8] **Deut 26:5** "And you shall make response before the Lord your God, 'A wandering Aramean was my father. And he went down into Egypt and sojourned there, few in number, and there he became a nation, great, mighty, and populous.'"

"Your name will be magnified forever…and the house of your serv-ant David will be established before you." (2 Sam 7:26)

David did not set upon the mercy and suck out the sweetness of it, look-ing no farther than his own comfort; no, he cared for no mercy except that God was magnified in it. So also, when God had delivered him from all his enemies, David proclaimed:

"The Lord is my rock and my fortress and my deliverer, my God, my rock, in whom I take refuge, my shield, and the horn of my sal-vation, my stronghold." (Ps 18:2)

Past saints did not put the crown on their own heads as we do.

For others, the mercies of God have been melting mercies, melting their souls in love to the God of their mercies. When Hannah received the mercy of a son, she said:

"My heart exults in the Lord; my horn is exalted in the Lord." (1 Sam 2:1)

This phrase suggests making more room for God. Past saints' hearts were not contracted but even more enlarged to God.

The mercies of God have also been mighty restraints to keep others from sin:

"Seeing that you, our God, have punished us less than our iniquities deserved and have given us such a remnant as this, shall we break your commandments again?" (Ezra 9:13-14)

Insightful souls have felt the force of the obligations of love and mercy upon them.

To conclude, God's mercies toward others have been like oil for the wheels of their obedience that makes them fitter for service (2 Chron 17:5).[9] Now, if the same mercies have the opposite effect on our hearts, what cause do we have to think that they do not come to us in love? I tell you, this is enough to dampen any of our spirits, to see what sweet effects God's mercies have had on others and what sad effects on us.

---

[9] **2 Chron 17:5** "Therefore the Lord established the kingdom in his hand. And all Judah brought tribute to Jehoshaphat, and he had great riches and honor."

Chapter 4

A Season of Adversity

The second special season in the life of a Christian that requires more than common diligence to keep the heart is a *time of adversity*. When providence frowns on you and blasts your outward comforts, then look to your hearts. Keep them with all diligence from complaining against God or fainting under His hand. For troubles, though sanctified, are still troubles; even rose bushes and holly thistles have their prickles.

Jonah was a good man, and yet how petulant his heart was under affliction. Job was the mirror of patience, yet how discomposed his heart was by trouble. You will find it as hard to get a composed spirit under great afflictions as it is to fix mercury in its place. Afflictions cause panic and confusion even in the best of hearts!

Therefore, the second question is: *how can we keep our heart from complaining or despairing under the hand of God in great afflictions*? I will offer nine special considerations here to keep your heart in these circumstances.

Afflictions are for our good

First, work this great truth on your hearts: by these difficult providences, God is faithfully pursuing the great design of electing love on our souls, and He orders all of our trials as instruments of sanctification to that end.

Afflictions do not happen by *causality* but by *counsel* (Job 5:6;[1] Eph 1:11[2]). They are ordained by the counsel of God to be a means of spiritual good for saints:

> *"He disciplines us for our good, that we may share his holiness."*
> *(Heb 12:10)*

> *"And we know that for those who love God all things work together for good, for those who are called according to his purpose."*
> *(Rom 8:28)*

Afflictions are God's workmen acting on our hearts to pull down our pride and security in the flesh. Because they are used this way, their nature is changed, and they are turned into blessings and benefits:

> *"It is good for me that I was afflicted, that I might learn your statutes." (Ps 119:71)*

Therefore, you certainly have no reason to complain. Instead, admire that God should concern Himself so much in your good that He

---

[1] **Job 5:6** "For affliction does not come from the dust, nor does trouble sprout from the ground."

[2] **Eph 1:11** "In him we have obtained an inheritance, having been predestined according to the purpose of him who works all things according to the counsel of his will."

will use any means necessary to accomplish it. Paul could praise God if "by any means possible [he] may attain the resurrection from the dead" (Phil 3:11). James said, "count it all joy, my brothers, when you meet trials of various kinds" (James 1:2). Say to yourself:

> *My Father is working a design of love on my soul, and do I do well to be angry with Him? All that He does is in pursuit of and reference to some eternal, glorious purpose for my soul. Oh, it is my ignorance of God's design that makes me quarrel with Him!*

He says to you in this case as He did to Peter: "What I am doing you do not understand now, but afterward you will understand" (John 13:7).

God's steadfast love

Though God has reserved the right to afflict His people, yet He has tied up His own hands by a promise to never take away His lovingkindness from them.

> *"I will be to him a father, and he shall be to me a son. When he commits iniquity, I will discipline him with the rod of men, with the stripes of the sons of men, but my steadfast love will not depart from him." (2 Sam 7:14)*

Can I look that Scripture in the face with a bitter, discontent spirit? Oh, my heart, my proud heart! When God has given you the whole tree with all the clusters of comfort growing on it, do you do well to complain because He permits the wind to blow down a few leaves? Christians have two sorts of possessions, the eternal goods of the throne and the passing goods of the footstool; if God has secured the former, never let my heart be troubled at the loss of the latter. Indeed, if He had cut off

His love or disowned my soul, I would have reason to be cast down; but this He has not done.

God has ordained our afflictions

One very effective way to keep the heart from sinking under afflictions is to call to mind that your own Father is ordaining them. Not a creature moves hand or tongue against you except by His permission. Suppose your cup is bitter, yet it is the cup that your Father has given you to drink. And can you suspect poison to be in the cup that He hands you?

Apply this case to your own heart and to your own experience; can you find it in your heart to give your child something that would hurt and undo them? No, you would as soon hurt yourself as your child.

"If you then, who are evil, know how to give good gifts to your children, how much more will your Father?" (Matt 7:11)

He is a God of love, pity, and tender mercies, and He relates to you as a father, husband, and friend. This consideration of His nature might be security enough, even if He had not spoken a word to comfort you in this case; and yet, you have His word too: "I will do you no harm" (Jer 25:6). You lie too near to His heart for Him to hurt you, and nothing grieves Him more than your soundless and unworthy suspicions of His designs. Would it not grieve a faithful and tender-hearted physician, when he had studied the case of his patient and prepared the most excellent remedies to save his life, to hear him cry out, *"Oh, he has undone me and poisoned me,"* because it pains him in the operation? Oh, what will it take to trust Him?

God regards us in suffering

God regards you as much in a low condition as in a high one; therefore, it should not trouble you so much to be made low. No, to be honest, He manifests more of His love, grace, and tenderness in a time of affliction than prosperity. Just as God did not first choose you because you were high, so He will also not forsake you because you are low. Men may look down on you and alter their regard for you as your condition is altered. When providence has blasted your estates, your summer friends may grow distant, fearing you may be a burden to them. But will God do so? No, never!

"I will never leave you nor forsake you." (Heb 13:5)

Indeed, if adversity and poverty could bar you from access to God, it would be a sad condition; but you can go to God as freely as ever.

"But as for me, I will look to the Lord;
I will wait for the God of my salvation;
my God will hear me." (Mic 7:7)

Poor David, when he was stripped of all earthly comforts, could yet encourage himself in the Lord his God, and why can't you? Suppose your husband or child had lost everything at sea and returned home to you in rags; would you deny their relation? Would you refuse to see them? If you would not, how much less will God? Why, then, are you so troubled? Although your condition has changed, your Father's love and respect have not!

Afflictions remove worldly temptations

And what if by the loss of your outward comforts, God preserves your soul from the ruining power of temptation? Then you certainly have little cause for your heart to sink by such sad thoughts about your trials. Are not these earthly enjoyments the things that make us shrink and fall in times of trial? Many have forsaken Christ in such an hour for the love of these things.

"The rich young ruler went away sorrowful, for he had great possessions." (Matt 19:22)

So, if this is God's design, what do you gain by quarreling with Him? Mariners in a storm can throw overboard rich bales of silk and other precious things to preserve their vessel and their lives as well, and everyone will approve of their actions. We also know that soldiers in a besieged city can demolish or burn the best buildings outside the walls to deny their enemies a place for shelter, and no one doubts that this is wisely done. People with gangrened legs or arms can willingly stretch them out to be amputated—not only thanking but paying the surgeon for his time. And must you grumble against God for casting over what would sink you in a storm; for pulling down that which would give your enemy an advantage in the siege of temptation; and for cutting off what would endanger your everlasting life? Oh, ungrateful child! Are not the things that you grieve for the very things that have ruined thousands of souls? What Christ is doing with your afflictions now, you do not know, but afterward, you will understand.

Afflictions can be an answer to prayer

It would also calm our hearts under adversity to consider that God, using such humbling providences, may be accomplishing the very thing that you have long prayed and waited for. And should you be troubled by that? Tell me, Christian, do you not have many prayers offered before God on such accounts as these: that He would keep you from sin; that He would reveal the emptiness and insufficiency of the flesh; that He would kill and mortify your lusts; and that your heart may never find rest in any enjoyment but Christ? In fact, by such humbling and impoverishing strokes, God may be fulfilling your desires. Would you be kept from sin? Look, He has hedged up your way with thorns (Hos 2:6)![3] Would you see the emptiness of the flesh? Your affliction is a fair glass to discover it; for the insufficiency of the flesh is never so effectively and sensibly discovered as it is in our own experience of it. Would you have your corruptions mortified? This is the way: God takes away the food and fuel that maintains them. For just as prosperity conceived and fed them, so also adversity, when sanctified, is a means to kill them. Would you have your heart to rest in no place other than the bosom of God? What better way can you imagine providence to take to answer your prayer than by pulling from under your head that soft pillow of worldly delights on which you rest? And yet, peevish child, how you fret at this and exercise your Father's patience! If He delays answering your prayers, you are ready to say He does not care for you. If He does that which really answers the scope and main goal of them but not in the way you expected, you quarrel with Him for that, as if instead of answering, He were thwarting all your hopes and aims. Is this wise? Is it not enough that God is so gracious to do what you ask, but you must be so bold as to expect that He should do it in the way that you prescribe?

---

[3] **Hos 2:6** "Therefore I will hedge up her way with thorns, and I will build a wall against her, so that she cannot find her paths."

Suffering has a future design

Again, it may comfort your heart to consider that in these troubles, God is accomplishing His plans; and if you could see the design of them, your soul would rejoice. We poor creatures are burdened with much ignorance, unable to discern how particular providences work toward God's purpose for them. As a result, like Israel in the wilderness, we are often murmuring because providence leads us about in a howling desert where we are exposed to difficulties. But He led them, and is now leading us, "by the right way…to a city of habitation" (Ps 107:7).[4] God in His secret counsel has exactly laid the whole plot and design of your salvation even to the smallest means and circumstances:

> *This way, and by these means alone shall you be saved. This number of afflictions I appoint for you at this time and in this order. They will come upon you and in this way, they will work for your good.*

If you could only discern the admirable harmony of divine workings and their mutual relations to each other—together with their connection and influence on the end result—of all the conditions in the world, you would choose the one that you are in now if you had the liberty to make your own choice. Providence is like a unique mosaic made up of thousands of pieces; we do not know what to make out of any one piece, but when put together and connected in an orderly way, they present a beautiful history to our eyes.

God works all things according to the counsel of His own will, and, therefore, that counsel of God has ordained this as the best way to bring about your salvation. For Christians with proud hearts, God appoints the right number of humbling circumstances for them. For others with

---

[4] Ps 107:7 "And he led them forth by the right way, that they might go to a city of habitation." (KJV)

worldly hearts, He appoints impoverishing providences. If you could only see this, I would not need to say more to support the most dejected heart.

Discontent is worse than the suffering

Furthermore, it would greatly comfort your hearts to consider that by fretting and complaining you do yourself more injury than is done by any of your current afflictions. Your own discontent is that which arms your troubles with a sting; and it is you that makes your burden heavy by struggling under it. If you could just lie quietly under the hand of God, your condition would be much easier and sweeter than it is. But your resistance makes God apply more strokes, as a Father would do on a stubborn child that does not receive correction.

Besides, this makes the soul unfit to pray over its troubles or to sense the good that God intends by them. Affliction is a pill, which, being wrapped up in patience and quiet submission, may be easily swallowed. But discontent chews the pill and so embitters the soul. God throws away some comfort which he saw would hurt you, and you throw away your peace after it. He shoots an arrow that sticks in your clothes to frighten you from sin, not to hurt you, and you thrust it deeper to the piercing of your very heart by despondency and discontent.

The plight of the unsaved

Lastly, if all this will not work, and your heart, like Rachel's,[5] still refuses to be comforted or quieted, then consider one more thing that,

---

[5] Jer 31:15 "Thus says the Lord: 'A voice is heard in Ramah, lamentation and bitter weeping. Rachel is weeping for her children; she refuses to be comforted for her children, because they are no more.'"

if seriously considered, will doubtlessly do the work: *Compare the condition you are now in (and are so much dissatisfied with) with the condition that others are in.* Others are roaring in flames and howling under the scourge of vengeance, and we deserve to be among them. Say to yourself:

> *Oh, my soul! Is this hell? Is my condition as bad as the damned? Oh, what would thousands now in hell give to change conditions with me?*

Doctor Taylor gives us a famous account of the Duke of Conde. He recalls that when the Duke had entered voluntarily into a vow of religious poverty, he was one day seen and pitied by a Lord of Italy. Out of tender kindness, this Lord wished him to be more careful and caring of his person. But the Duke said, "Sir, do not be troubled, and do not think that I am lacking in conveniences, for I send a harbinger before me who prepares my lodgings and ensures that I am royally entertained." The Lord asked him who was this harbinger? He answered, "The knowledge of myself and the consideration of the eternal torment that I deserve for my sins. When I arrive at my lodging with this knowledge, no matter how lacking I find it, I think it is even better than I deserve."

Therefore, why does the living Christian complain? In this way, the heart may be kept from despairing or complaining under adversity.

Chapter 5

A Season of Church Troubles

The third season calling for more than ordinary diligence in keeping the heart is during a time of trouble for the Church. The Church is like the boat that carried Christ and His disciples across the sea (Matt 8:23-27); when it is oppressed and ready to perish in the waves of persecution, then many good souls are also ready to sink and be shipwrecked upon the billows of their own fear.

I confess that most saints need the spur rather than the reins in this case, for some sit down completely overwhelmed with a sense of the Church's troubles. The loss of the Ark cost Eli his life (1 Sam 4:18),[1] and the sad condition of Jerusalem made good Nehemiah's countenance change in the midst of all the pleasures and accommodations of the court (Neh 2:2).[2] The Church's troubles affect even the best of hearts!

---

[1] **1 Sam 4:18** "As soon as he mentioned the ark of God, Eli fell over backward from his seat by the side of the gate, and his neck was broken and he died, for the man was old and heavy. He had judged Israel forty years."

[2] **Neh 2:2** "And the king said to me, 'Why is your face sad, seeing you are not sick? This is nothing but sadness of the heart.'"

God allows, indeed commands, us to be alert and aware of these calamities, calling for a day of "weeping and mourning, for baldness and wearing sackcloth" (Isa 22:12) and severely warning those who are unaware (Amos 6:1).[3] Yet, it will not please him to see you sit like Elijah despairing under the Juniper tree, who said, "It is enough; now, O Lord, take away my life" (1 Kings 19:4). You may, and ought, to be mourners in Zion, but self-tormentors you must not be. Complain *to* God, but do not complain *of* God, which includes how you carry yourself and the language of your actions.

So, how can open and tender hearts be relieved and supported when they are weighed down with a burdensome sense of the Church's troubles? For those who prefer the Church over other joys, I know it is hard to keep your hearts from sinking down under the weight of its troubles. And yet, this can and should be done by applying the following heart-establishing considerations.

God is in control

Settle this great truth in your hearts, that no trouble comes upon the Church but by the permission of her God; and He permits nothing that will not also bring much good in the end to His people.

There is truly a principle of resting in both the permitting and the commanding will of God. This can be seen in David, "Leave him alone…for the Lord has told him to" (2 Sam 16:11), and in Christ, "You would have no authority over me at all unless it had been given you from above" (John 19:11). It should greatly calm our spirits to know that it is the will of God to permit it; and if He had not permitted it, it could never have been as it is.

---

[3] **Amos 6:1** "Woe to those who are at ease in Zion, and to those who feel secure on the mountain of Samaria, the notable men of the first of the nations, to whom the house of Israel comes!"

This very consideration quieted Job, Eli, David, and Hezekiah—the fact that the Lord did it was enough for them. And why should it not be so for us? If the Lord allows the Church to be plowed as a field (Jer 26:18)[4] and her beautiful stones to lie in the dust (Ezek 26:12);[5] if it is His decision that the Antichrist will rage longer and wear out the saints of the Most High (Dan 7:25);[6] if it is His will for "a day of tumult and trampling and confusion in the valley of vision" (Isa 22:5); or if He permits the wicked to devour a man who is more righteous (Hab 1:13),[7] who are we that we should argue with God? Rather, we should be resigned to the will of the One who created us, and He who made us should use us as He pleases. He may do what seems good to Him without our consent. Does lowly man stand on equal ground that he should argue with his Creator or that God should render an account to him of any of His ways? In every way, it is reasonable that we should be content however God uses us and that we should be obedient to whatever He commands us.

But let us pursue this argument even further by considering that all of God's permissions eventually result in the real good of His people. This fact will quiet our spirits even more. Do enemies carry away the

---

[4] **Jer 26:18** "Zion shall be plowed as a field; Jerusalem shall become a heap of ruins, and the mountain of the house a wooded height."

[5] **Ezek 26:12** "They will plunder your riches and loot your merchandise. They will break down your walls and destroy your pleasant houses. Your stones and timber and soil they will cast into the midst of the waters."

[6] **Dan 7:25** "He shall speak words against the Most High, and shall wear out the saints of the Most High, and shall think to change the times and the law; and they shall be given into his hand for a time, times, and half a time."

[7] **Hab 1:13** "You who are of purer eyes than to see evil and cannot look at wrong, why do you idly look at traitors and remain silent when the wicked swallows up the man more righteous than he?"

best among God's people into captivity? This looks like a sad providence, and yet, God sends them there for their good (Jer 24:5).[8] Does God take the Assyrians as a staff in His hand to beat His people with? Those blows are painful and make them cry, but His purpose is to finish "all his work on Mount Zion" (Isa 10:12).[9] If God can bring much good out of the worst and greatest evil of sin, how much more can He accomplish out of temporary afflictions? It is clear that He can do so and, moreover, that He will. For it is inconsistent with the wisdom of any individual to permit anything (which he might prevent if he pleased) to hinder his great design and purpose. So, it cannot be imagined that our wise God should do so.

Therefore, as Luther told Melanchthon, so I say to you: let infinite wisdom, power, and love alone; for by these, all creatures are swayed, and all actions are guided with regard to the Church. It is not our work to rule the world but to submit to Him who does. The motions of Providence are all judicious and the wheels are full of eyes;[10] it is enough that the Church's affairs are in good hands.

God is with us

When considering the Church's troubles, ponder this heart-supporting truth: No matter how many troubles are forever upon her, yet her King is in her.

---

[8] **Jer 24:5** "Thus saith the Lord, the God of Israel; Like these good figs, so will I acknowledge them that are carried away captive of Judah, whom I have sent out of this place into the land of the Chaldeans for their good." (KJV)

[9] **Isa 10:12** "When the Lord has finished all his work on Mount Zion and on Jerusalem, he will punish the speech of the arrogant heart of the king of Assyria and the boastful look in his eyes."

[10] The imagery of wheels with eyes is taken from Ezekiel's vision in Ezekiel 10.

What, has the Lord forsaken His churches? Has He sold them into the enemy's hand? Does He not see the evil that befalls them? Are these doubts the reason that our hearts sink so fast? This is a shameful undervaluing of our great God; we magnify poor, impotent man and flee and tremble at creatures while God is in the midst of us. It is true that the Church's enemies are many and mighty, yet that argument that Caleb and Joshua used to raise their own hearts is just as effective now as it was then:

"The Lord is with us; do not fear them." (Num 14:9)

The Historian tells us that when Antigonus overheard his soldiers in great discouragement reckoning the size of the enemy army, he suddenly stepped in among them with this question, "and how many do you reckon me for?" Discouraged souls, how many do you reckon the Lord for? Does He not far outmatch any enemy, and is not the Almighty more than many mighty men? Does His presence account for nothing with us?

"If God is for us, who can be against us?" (Rom 8:31)

What do you think was the reason for Gideon's tests of God in Judges 6? He questions (v. 12-13), asks for a sign (v. 17), and after that another (v. 36). And what was ultimately the purpose for these tests but to be sure that the Lord was with him and that he might write this motto upon his ensign, "A sword for the Lord and for Gideon" (Judg 7:20). So, if you can be assured that the Lord is with His people, you will then be able to get above all your discouragements. And you do not need to look for a sign from heaven because, in fact, you have a sign before you—the marvelous preservation of His people amidst all their enemies. If God is not with his people, how is it that they are not quickly swallowed up? Do their enemies lack malice, power, or opportunity? No, but there is an invisible hand on them. Well then, as it was with the Israelites, let God's presence give us rest (Ex 33:14).[11]

> *"Therefore we will not fear though the earth gives way,*
> *though the mountains be moved into the heart of the sea." (Ps 46:2)*

God is in the midst of His Church; she shall not be moved!

Suffering helps the Church

Ponder the great benefits for the people of God who are experiencing affliction. If a low and afflicted state in the world is really best for the Church, then your dejections are not only irrational but ungrateful. Indeed, if you estimate the happiness of the Church by its worldly ease, splendor, and prosperity, then such times will seem bad for her; but if you reckon its glory to consist in its humility, faith, patience, and heavenly-mindedness, no condition in the world is more advantageous for these as an afflicted condition. It was not persecution and prisons, but worldliness and carelessness that was the poison of the Church. Neither was it the earthly glory of its *members*, but the blood of its *martyrs* that was the seed of the Church. The power of godliness never thrived better than in affliction, and it never ran lower than in times of greatest prosperity. When we are left "humble and lowly," then we will "seek refuge in the name of the Lord" (Zeph 3:12).[12] What do you say? Is it not advantageous for the saints to be weaned from the loves and delights of ensnaring worldly vanities? Should we not long to be hastened and pushed forward with more speed to heaven to find our promised rest?

---

[11] **Ex 33:14** " And he said, 'My presence will go with you, and I will give you rest.'"

[12] **Zeph 3:12** "But I will leave in your midst a people humble and lowly. They shall seek refuge in the name of the Lord."

Should we not want clearer discoveries of our own hearts and to be taught to pray more fervently, frequently, and spiritually? Experience teaches us that if these things are best for us, then there is no condition so naturally blessed with such fruits than an afflicted condition.

And is it proper, then, to complain and sulk because your Father concerns Himself more with the health of your soul than He does to please your whims? Do you resent that He will bring you closer to heaven than you are willing to go? Is this a proper return for the love of God, who is so pleased to concern Himself with your welfare? And this is more than He will do for thousands in the world who lack any disciplinary afflictions from His hand for their good (Hos 4:17;[13] Matt 15:14[14]). But alas! We judge by our senses, reckoning things good or evil according to what we, in the moment, can see and feel in them.

God continues to bless

Take care to not overlook the many precious mercies that you enjoy from God in the midst of all your troubles. It is a pity that our tears on account of our troubles should so blur and blind our eyes that we do not see our blessings and the grounds of our comfort. I will not insist upon the mercy of having your lives given to you as a gift, nor upon the many outward comforts, everyday conveniences, and homes, which go beyond what Christ and His precious servants (of whom the world was not worthy) ever had.

But how much do we value pardon from sin, interest in Christ, the covenant of promises, and an eternity of happiness in the presence of God at the end of our few days on earth? Oh! How can we, who are

---

[13] **Hos 4:17** "Ephraim is joined to idols; leave him alone."

[14] **Matt 15:14** "Let them alone; they are blind guides. And if the blind lead the blind, both will fall into a pit."

entitled to such mercies as these, droop under any temporary afflictions? Why should we concern ourselves over the frowns of others and the loss of our possessions? You may not have the smiles of the powerful, but you have the favor of your great God. You may have losses in your investments but corresponding improvements in your spiritual life. If you cannot live as courageously, securely, and easily as before, you still may live as holy and heavenly as ever. Will you then grieve so much for these incidentals that you forget your essentials? Will light troubles make you forget weighty mercies? Remember the Church's true riches are laid out of reach of all its enemies, who can make you poor but not miserable. So what if God does not distinguish His outward blessings between His own people and others? What if His judgments single out the best and spare the worst? An Abel is killed in love, but a Cain survives in hatred;[15] a bloody Dionysius dies in his bed,[16] but a good Josiah falls in battle.[17] Even if the belly of the wicked is filled with hidden treasures and the teeth of the saints are broken on gravel, yet still there is much for which to praise; for electing love has distinguished, even if common providence has not. And just as prosperity and license will slay the wicked, even death and adversity will benefit and save the righteous.

Christ's Church will prevail

Believe that no matter how low the Church is plunged under the waters of adversity, she will assuredly rise again. Fear not, for as sure as Christ rose on the third day—despite the sealed stone and watch on His tomb—so also the Church will rise out of all her troubles and lift up her

---

[15] See Genesis 4:1-16.

[16] Possibly referring to Dionysius I, a Greek tyrant of Syracuse.

[17] Josiah was a good king of Judah who died in battle. See 2 Chron 35:23-24.

victorious head above all her enemies. There is no fear of ruining a people who survive by their losses and multiply by being diminished. Oh, be not too quick to bury the Church before she is dead! Stay until Christ has tried His skill before you give her up for lost; the bush may be engulfed in flames, but it will never be consumed—and that is owing to the goodwill of Him who dwells in the bush!

Consider the famous instances of God's care and tenderness over His people in former trials. Christ has not permitted them to be devoured. Although the Christian Church has lived in affliction for the past 1600 years, yet she is not consumed. Many waves of persecution have gone over her, and yet she is not drowned; there have been many designs to ruin her, and to this point, none have succeeded. This is not the first time that *Hamans*[18] and *Ahitophels*[19] have plotted her ruin or that a *Herod*[20] has stretched out his hand to thwart her. Still, the Church has been preserved from, supported under, or delivered out of all her troubles. And is she not as dear to God as ever? Is He not as able to save her now as formerly? Though we know not how our deliverance will arise, yet "the Lord knows how to rescue the godly from trials" (2 Pet 2:9).

Concern for the Church is commendable

If you can gain no comfort from any of the former arguments, then, in the last place, see whether you cannot draw some comfort out of your actual concern. Surely, this concern of yours is a good argument for your integrity. Union is the ground of sympathy; if you did not have some rich experience in that ship, you would not tremble as you do

---

[18] Referring to Haman's plot to kill the Jews in Esther. See Esther 3.

[19] Ahithophel counseled Absalom how to defeat David and his men. See 2 Samuel 17.

[20] Herod attempted to kill the Christ child. See Matthew 2.

when it is in danger of sinking. Besides, this frame of spirit may supply you with this encouragement: if you are so aware of the Church's troubles, Jesus Christ is much more aware and concerned about her than you could ever be. And He will cast an eye of favor upon those who mourn for her (Isa 57:18).[21]

---

[21] **Isa 57:18** "I have seen his ways, but I will heal him; I will lead him and restore comfort to him and his mourner."

Chapter 6

A Season of Fear

The fourth special season that requires the utmost diligence to keep the heart is during a time of public danger and calamity. In such times, even the best hearts are only too apt to be surprised by slavish fear.

It is not easy to secure the heart against distraction in times of destruction:

> "When the house of David was told, 'Syria is in league with Ephraim,' the heart of Ahaz and the heart of his people shook as the trees of the forest shake before the wind." (Isa 7:2)

> "And there will be signs in sun and moon and stars, and on the earth distress of nations in perplexity because of the roaring of the sea and the waves, people fainting with fear and with foreboding of what is coming on the world. For the powers of the heavens will be shaken." (Luke 21:25-26)

Even Paul himself sometimes complains of "fighting without and fear within" (2 Cor 7:5).[1]

But, my brothers, these things should not be so; saints should be of a more uplifted spirit. This was the case with David when his heart was kept in a good frame:

> *"The Lord is my light and my salvation; whom shall I fear? The Lord is the stronghold of my life; of whom shall I be afraid?"*
> *(Ps 27:1)*

Let none but the servants of sin be the slaves of fear; let only those who have delighted in evil fear evil. Oh, do not let that which God has threatened as a judgment on the wicked ever seize upon the breasts of the righteous.

> *"I will send faintness into their hearts in the lands of their enemies. The sound of a driven leaf shall put them to flight." (Lev 26:36)*

What poor-spirited men were these, to fly at a shaking leaf, which makes a pleasant noise, rather than a terrible one, and is itself a kind of natural music. But to a guilty conscience, the rustling leaves are drums and trumpets. However,

> *"God gave us a spirit not of fear but of power and love and self-control." (2 Tim 1:7)*

---

[1] **2 Cor 7:5** "For even when we came into Macedonia, our bodies had no rest, but we were afflicted at every turn—fighting without and fear within."

A sound mind that stands in contrast to the spirit of fear is a clean conscience that is not burdened by guilt. And this should make us as bold as a lion!

I know it cannot be said of a saint what God said of the Leviathan, that he was a "creature without fear" (Job 41:33). There is natural fear in all of us, and it is impossible to be wholly rid of it, as our minds are subject to anxieties, rising from the apprehension of approaching danger. So long as dangers can approach us, we will find some anxieties within us. It is not my purpose to advise you to adopt an apathetic stoicism. Neither do I want to dissuade you from an appropriate degree of caution and preventative fear that may equip you for troubles and be serviceable to your souls. There is a judicious fear that opens our eyes to foresee danger, motivating us to prudent and lawful means to prevent it (such was Jacob's fear as he prepared to meet Esau[2]). But this is a controlled and wise fear. I plead with you to keep your hearts from the tyrannical passions that invade the heart in times of danger. This type of fear distracts, weakens, and unfits the heart for duty; it is accompanied by a snare and drives men to pursue unlawful means.

The fourth question is: *how can we keep our hearts from distracting and tormenting fears in times of great and threatening dangers?* Now, there are fourteen excellent rules that can help you keep the heart from sinful fear when eminent dangers threaten you.

Rest in God's sovereignty

Consider that all creatures are in the hand of God, who manages them in all their ways—limiting, restraining, and determining them all as He pleases. Get this truth firmly settled in your heart by faith, and you will be marvelously guarded against slavish fears.

---

[2] See Genesis 32:1-21.

The first chapter of Ezekiel contains an admirable glimpse or representation of Providence; there you can see the living creatures who move the wheels, which are the great affairs and movements of things here below. They come to Christ on the throne to receive new orders and instructions from Him (v. 24-26).[3] And in Revelation 6, you read of white, black, and red horses, which are nothing else but the instruments that God employs in the execution of His judgments in the world—namely, wars, disease, and death. But when these horses are prancing and trampling up and down the world, here is the truth that can quiet our hearts: God has the reins in His hand! Wicked men are sometimes like mad horses; they would stamp the people of God under their feet except for the fact that the bridle of Providence is in their mouths (John 19:11-12).[4] A lion in the wild is terrible to meet, but who is afraid of the lion in the keeper's hand?

See God as your Father

Remember that this God, who holds all creatures in His hands, is your Father, and He is much more tender over you than you are—or ever could be—over yourselves.

---

[3] **Ezek 1:24-26** "And when they went, I heard the sound of their wings like the sound of many waters, like the sound of the Almighty, a sound of tumult like the sound of an army. When they stood still, they let down their wings. And there came a voice from above the expanse over their heads. When they stood still, they let down their wings. And above the expanse over their heads there was the likeness of a throne, in appearance like sapphire; and seated above the likeness of a throne was a likeness with a human appearance."

[4] **John 19:11** "Jesus answered him, 'You would have no authority over me at all unless it had been given you from above. Therefore he who delivered me over to you has the greater sin.'"

"He who touches you touches the apple of his eye." (Zech 2:8)

Let me ask the most timid woman whether there is not a vast difference between the sight of a drawn sword in the hand of a blood-thirsty ruffian and the same sword in the hand of her own tender husband. There is as great a difference in looking upon creatures with the eye of sense and looking on them with the eye of faith as being in the hand of your God. Consider this sweet scripture:

"For your Maker is your husband, the Lord of hosts is his name; and the Holy One of Israel is your Redeemer, the God of the whole earth he is called." (Isa 54:5)

He is Lord of all the hosts of creatures in the world. Should you be afraid to pass through an army, though all the soldiers should turn their swords and guns toward you, if the general of that army were your best friend or father?

I have come across an excellent story of a religious young man who was at sea in a storm with many other passengers who were half dead with fear. He was the only one who appeared cheerful, as if he were little concerned in that danger. One of the passengers demanded a reason for his cheerfulness, and he said, *"because the pilot of the ship is my father."* Consider Christ first as the King and Supreme Lord over the providential kingdom of God, and then see Him as your Head, Husband, and Friend. You will quickly say:

"Return, O my soul, to your rest." (Ps 116:7)[5]

---

[5] **Ps 116:7** "Return, O my soul, to your rest; for the Lord has dealt bountifully with you."

This truth will make you stop trembling and start singing in the midst of dangers. "For God is the King of all the earth; sing praises with a psalm" (Ps 47:7). Or, as the Hebrew text implies, everyone sings who understands this heart-reviving and establishing doctrine of the dominion of our Father over all creation.

Remember the commands of Christ

In these moments, set your heart on the express prohibitions of Christ, and let your heart stand in awe of the violations of them. He has charged you not to fear:

> "And when you hear of wars and tumults, do not be terrified."
> (Luke 21:9)

> "And not frightened in anything by your opponents."
> (Phil 1:28)

> "So have no fear of them, for nothing is covered that will not be revealed, or hidden that will not be known. And do not fear those who kill the body but cannot kill the soul. Rather fear him who can destroy both soul and body in hell. Fear not, therefore; you are of more value than many sparrows." (Matt 10:26,28,31)

In fact, within the compass of six verses in Matthew 10, our Savior commands us three times *not to fear man*. Does every word of proud dust and ashes make you afraid? Does the voice of a man make you tremble more than the voice of God? If you are of such a fearful and timid spirit, how is it that you do not fear to disobey the direct commands of Jesus Christ? I think that the command of Christ should have as much power to calm as the voice of a poor worm to terrify your heart.

"I, I am he who comforts you;
who are you that you are afraid of man who dies,
of the son of man who is made like grass,
and have forgotten the Lord, your Maker,
who stretched out the heavens
and laid the foundations of the earth."
(Isa 51:12-13)

We are not able to sinfully fear creatures until we have forgotten God; if we remembered what He is and what He has said, we would not be in such feeble spirits. Therefore, bring your heart to this decision in times of danger:

If I allow my heart to be enslaved by the fear of man, I must abandon the reverential awe and fear of God, and do I dare cast off the fear of the Almighty for the frowns of men? Will I lift up proud dust above the great God? Will I venture into certain sin to shun a possible danger?

Oh, keep your heart with that consideration!

Remember the futility of past fears

Think about how much needless trouble your past fears have brought you and how you have disquieted yourself for no reason.

"And you fear continually all the day
because of the wrath of the oppressor,
when he sets himself to destroy?
And where is the wrath of the oppressor?" (Isa 51:13)

The enemy seemed ready to destroy, and yet you are not destroyed; God has not brought upon you the thing that you feared, so you have wasted your spirit, disordered your soul, and weakened your hands— all to no purpose. You might have all this time enjoyed your peace and patiently kept your soul. And, here, I cannot fail to observe a very deep policy of Satan to manage a design against the soul with these vain fears. I call them vain in how they are thwarted by providence, but certainly, they are not in vain with respect to Satan's purpose in raising them. For here he acts like soldiers used to do in the siege of a garrison, who wore out their opponent by constant waiting and watching in order to weaken their resistance before choosing to storm them in earnest. Every night they sound out false alarms, and although this comes to nothing, it still notably furthers the design of the enemy. Oh, when will you beware of Satan's devices?

Fear sinful fear

Solemnly consider that though the things you fear might really happen, yet there is more evil in your own fear than in the thing feared. For the least evil of sin is worse than the greatest evil of suffering. This sinful fear often brings more torment and trouble than the condition that frightens you. In this state, fear is both a multiplying and a tormenting passion; it represents troubles much greater than they are so the soul is that much more tortured and wracked when the suffering itself comes.

This was true of Israel at the Red Sea when they cried out and were very afraid until they stepped into the water. They found a passage was opened through those waters that they thought would have drowned them. The same is true of us. We look through the glass of carnal fear upon the waters of trouble, the swelling waters of the Jordan, and we cry out that they are uncrossable and that we will certainly perish in them! But when we in fact come into the midst of those floodwaters, we find the promise holds: God will "provide the way of escape" (1 Cor 10:13). This was also true of blessed Thomas Bilney, who put his finger to the candle as a test but cried out, *"What? Cannot I bear the burning of a finger? How then will I be able to bear the burning of my whole body tomorrow?"*[6] And yet, when that day came, he was able to go cheerfully into the flames with that scripture in his mouth:

> *"Fear not, for I have redeemed you;*
> *I have called you by name, you are mine.*
> *When you pass through the waters, I will be with you;*
> *and through the rivers, they shall not overwhelm you;*
> *when you walk through fire you shall not be burned,*
> *and the flame shall not consume you." (Isa 43:1-2)*

Rest on God's promises

Consult the many precious promises which are written for your support and comfort in all dangers. These are your refuges to which you may fly and be safe when "the arrow...flies by day" and "destruction...wastes at noonday" (Ps 91:5-7).[7] There are particular promises that are suited to particular cases and urgent needs, and there are general promises that apply to all cases and conditions, such as the following passages:

---

[6] Thomas Bilney was a martyr of the reformation who died at the stake in 1531.

[7] **Ps 91:5-7** "You will not fear the terror of the night, nor the arrow that flies by day, nor the pestilence that stalks in darkness, nor the destruction that wastes at noonday. A thousand may fall at your side, ten thousand at your right hand, but it will not come near you."

"And we know that for those who love God all things work together for good, for those who are called according to his purpose."
(Rom 8:28)

"Though a sinner does evil a hundred times and prolongs his life, yet I know that it will be well with those who fear God, because they fear before him." (Eccl 8:12)

"Believe in the Lord your God, and you will be established."
(2 Chron 20:20)

If you could plead these promises with God as Jacob did you would find relief in every distress:

"But you said, 'I will surely do you good...'" (Gen 32:12)

You might object that this promise was made personally and by name to Jacob and not to you. But if Jacob's God is your God, then you have as good a share in these promises as he had. A thousand years after that transaction between God and Jacob, Hosea applied what God spoke as if it had been spoken to all of Israel: "He met God at Bethel, and there God spoke with us" (Hos 12:4).

Remember God's faithfulness

Quiet your trembling hearts by recounting and consulting your past experiences of the care and faithfulness of God in former distresses. These experiences are food for your faith in a wilderness period

(Ps 74:14).[8] In this way, David kept his heart in a time of danger (1 Sam 17:37),[9] as did Paul (2 Cor 1:10).[10] When Silentiarius was told that his enemies were plotting to take away his life, he sweetly answered, *"If God has not taken care of me, how have I escaped thus far?"*

You may plead with God using old experiences to procure new ones, for pleading with God for new deliverances is similar to pleading for new pardons. Now, note how Moses pleads with God on that account:

> *"Please pardon the iniquity of this people, according to the greatness of your steadfast love, just as you have forgiven this people, from Egypt until now." (Num 14:19)*

He does not say, as men do, *"Lord, this is the first time you have been troubled to sign their pardon."* Rather, he says, *"Lord, because you have pardoned them so often, I beg you to pardon them once again."* So, when you face new trials, say, *"Lord, you have often heard, helped, and saved in times of former fears; therefore, help me now again, for with You, redemption is plentiful, and your arm is not shortened!"*

Find courage in obedience

In times of danger, remind yourself that you are faithfully following God, and that will give you a holy courage.

---

[8] **Ps 74:14** "You crushed the heads of Leviathan; you gave him as food for the creatures of the wilderness."

[9] **1 Sam 17:37** "And David said, 'The Lord who delivered me from the paw of the lion and from the paw of the bear will deliver me from the hand of this Philistine.'"

[10] **2 Cor 1:10** "He delivered us from such a deadly peril, and he will deliver us. On him we have set our hope that he will deliver us again."

"Now who is there to harm you if you are zealous for what is good?"
(1 Pet 3:13)

And if anyone dares to attempt to harm you:

"Entrust [your] souls to a faithful Creator while doing good."
(1 Pet 4:19)

It was this consideration that raised Luther's spirits above all fear: *"In the case of God,"* he said, *"I ever am and ever shall be stout; here, I assume the title, cedo nulli (I yield to none)."* A good cause will bear up a believer's spirit bravely. Hear the words of a heathen to the shame of cowardly Christians. When Emperor Vespasian had commanded Fluidius Priscus to not come to the Senate (or if he did to only speak what he was told), the senator returned this noble answer: that as he was a Senator, it was appropriate that he should be at the Senate; and if while there he was required to give his advice, he would speak freely that which his conscience commanded him. When the Emperor threatened him, he answered, *"Did I ever tell you that I was immortal? Do what you will, and I will do what I ought; it is in your power to put me to death unjustly, and it is my power to die steadfastly."*

Righteousness is a breastplate, and the cause of God will pay all your expenses. Only those who are not true to God's calling should tremble at danger.

Repent of sin

Get your consciences sprinkled with the blood of Christ from all guilt, and that will set your hearts above all fear. It is guilt upon our consciences that softens our spirits and makes them cowardly. On the contrary, "the righteous are bold as a lion" (Prov 28:1).[11] It was the guilt in Cain's conscience that made him cry, "whoever finds me will kill me" (Gen 4:14). A guilty conscience is more terrified with imagined dangers than a pure conscience is with real ones. A guilty sinner carries a witness against himself in his own bosom. It was guilt that made Herod cry out: "This is John the Baptist. He has been raised from the dead" (Matt 14:2). Such a conscience is the Devil's anvil on which he fabricates all the swords and spears that the guilty sinner uses to pierce and wound himself. Guilt is to danger what fire is to gunpowder; a man does not need to fear walking among many barrels of gunpowder if he is not carrying a flame.

Exercise holy trust

In times of great distress, exercise holy trust. Make it your business to trust God with your life and comforts, and then your heart will be at rest about them. As David said,

"When I am afraid, I put my trust in you." (Ps 56:3)

If at any time a storm rises, go to the Lord and find shelter under the covering of His wings. Go to God in an act of faith and trust, and never doubt that He will secure you.

"You keep him in perfect peace whose mind is stayed on you, because he trusts in you." (Isa 26:3)

---

[11] **Prov 28:1** "The wicked flee when no one pursues, but the righteous are bold as a lion."

89

God is pleased when you come to Him in this way:

Father, my life, liberty, and possessions are being hunted, and I cannot secure them; Oh, let me leave them in Your hand. The poor commits himself to you, and does God fail him? No, "you have been the helper of the fatherless" (Ps 10:14). That is, You are the helper of the one who is destitute, who has no one to go to but God.

And it is a sweet scripture that says, "He is not afraid of bad news; his heart is firm, trusting in the Lord" (Ps 112:7). He does not say that he is kept from the report of bad news (he may hear as sad of news as anyone may), but his heart will be kept from the terror of that news; "his heart is firm."

Adorn the gospel

In these times, consider the honor of the Christian faith more and your personal safety less. Do you think it is for the honor of the faith that Christians should be as fearful as hares, jumping at every sound? Will this not tempt the world to think that, despite what you say, your principles are no better than others? Oh, consider the possible damage done to others who observe your fears.

It was a noble saying of Nehemiah: "Should such a man as I run away? And what man such as I could go into the temple and live?" (Neh 6:11). Would it not be better for you to die than that the world should be prejudiced against Christ by your example? Alas! The world judges far more by what they see in your practices than by what they understand of your principles. How apt the world is to conclude from your fearfulness that, however much you commend faith and talk of assurance, you dare not trust these things any more than they do when put to the test. Oh, do not let your fears lay such a stumbling block before the blind world!

Rest in your eternal inheritance

If you will secure your heart from fear, you must first secure the eternal welfare of your soul in the hands of Jesus Christ. When this is done, then you may say, *"Now, world, do your worst!"* You will not be very concerned with your lowly body the moment you are assured that it will be well for all eternity with your precious soul. "Do not fear those," says Christ, "who kill the body, and after that have nothing more that they can do" (Luke 12:4). Assured Christians can smile with contempt upon all of their enemies and say, *"Is this the worst you can do?"*

What about you, Christians? Are you assured that your souls are safe and that within a few moments of your dissolution you will be received by Christ into everlasting life? Well, if you are sure of that, then never trouble yourselves about the instruments and means of your dissolution.

You could object and point out that a violent death is terrifying to our nature. But what difference is it to your soul in Heaven whether it left from your mouth or from your throat? Why does it matter whether it was your family, friends, or murderous enemies who stood around your dead body and closed your eyes? Alas! It is not worth making so much fuss about. Your soul will not be aware in Heaven how your body is being treated on Earth; rather, it will be swallowed up in life.

Fear the Lord

Learn to quench all enslaving earthly fears in the reverential fear of God. This is a cure by diversion. It is a rare piece of Christian wisdom to turn those predominating passions of the soul into spiritual channels—to turn natural anger into spiritual zeal, natural mirth into holy cheerfulness, and natural fear into a holy fear and awe of God. Christ Himself prescribes this method of cure in the previously mentioned verses in Matt 10:28, which is similar to what is written in Isaiah:

"Do not fear what they fear, nor be in dread." (Isa 8:12)

But how will we help it? In this way:

"But the Lord of hosts, him you shall honor as holy. Let him be your fear, and let him be your dread" (Isa 8:13).

Natural fear may be calmed for the moment by natural reason or the removal of the cause, but this is like a flame blown out with a whiff of air that is easily blown into flame again. But if the fear of God extinguishes it, then it is like a flame doused in water, which cannot easily be rekindled.

Pray

Lastly, take any fears that are poured upon you by the Devil and your own unbelief, and pour them out to God in prayer. Prayer is the best outlet for fear! What Christian cannot accept this proven remedy? I will give you the greatest example in the world to encourage you to pray, which is the example of Jesus Christ:

"And they went to a place called Gethsemane. And he said to his disciples, 'Sit here while I pray.' And he took with him Peter and James and John, and began to be greatly distressed and troubled."
(Mark 14:32-33)

When the hour of His danger and death drew near, He enters the garden, separates from the Disciples, and then wrestles mightily with God in prayer, even to the point of agony.

"In the days of his flesh, Jesus offered up prayers and supplications, with loud cries and tears, to him who was able to save him from death, and he was heard because of his reverence." (Heb 5:7)

He was heard regarding the strength and support He needed to carry Him through it, though not in deliverance or exemption from it.

Oh, that these things might abide with you and be put into practice in these evil days so that your trembling souls would be established by them!

Chapter 7

A Season of Need

The fifth season where you must exert diligence in keeping the heart is in a time of need and external pressing wants. During such times, we should complain *to* God and not *of* God (the throne of grace being erected for such a time of need[1]). Yet, when the waters of relief run low and wants begin to pinch hard, how prone are the best hearts to distrust the Fountain! When the grain in the barrel and the oil in the vessel are almost spent, our faith and patience are almost spent too.

Now, it is difficult at these times to keep the proud and unbelieving heart in a holy, quiet, and sweet submission at the foot of God. It is an easy thing to talk of trusting God for daily bread while we have a full barn or bank; but to say as this prophet, "though the fig tree should not blossom, nor fruit be on the vines…yet I will rejoice in the Lord" (Hab 3:17-18),[2] this is not easy!

---

[1] **Heb 4:16** "Let us then with confidence draw near to the throne of grace, that we may receive mercy and find grace to help in time of need."

[2] **Hab 3:17-18** "Though the fig tree should not blossom, nor fruit be on the vines, the produce of the olive fail and the fields yield no food, the flock be cut off from the fold and there be no herd in the stalls, yet I will rejoice in the Lord; I will take joy in the God of my salvation."

Therefore, the fifth question is: *how can we keep our hearts from distrusting God or bitterly complaining against Him when outward wants are either felt or feared?* This question deserves to be seriously considered and studied, especially now. Lately, it seems to be the design of Providence to withdraw earthly comforts from the people of God and acquaint them with trials that, until now, they have been altogether strangers to.

Now, to secure the heart from the previously mentioned danger that attends this condition, the following considerations may prove effective through the blessing of the Spirit.

You share the experience of past saints

Consider that if God has reduced you to little but basic necessities, He deals no differently with you than He has done with some of the best and holiest saints who have ever lived. Your condition is not unique, even if you have been strangers to wants until now. Other saints have had daily experiences of need.

Listen to what blessed Paul speaks, not of himself only, but in the names of other saints reduced to similar hardships:

> *"To the present hour we hunger and thirst, we are poorly dressed and buffeted and homeless." (1 Cor 4:11)*

Imagine such a man as Paul going up and down the world with tattered clothes, an empty belly, and no house in which to rest his head. He was so far above you in grace and holiness, doing more service for God in a day than perhaps you have done in a lifetime, and yet, you complain as if you are severely dealt with!

Have you forgotten what hardships and adversity even David suffered? How great were his trials? In his need, he said to Nabal, "give whatever you have at hand to your servants and to your son David" (1 Sam 25:8).

Renowned Musculus was forced to dig in the town's ditch for maintenance. Famous Ainsworth (as I have been credibly informed) was forced to sell his own bed to buy bread. But why should I speak of these? Behold one who is greater than any of them: the only Son of God! He is "the heir of all things, through whom also he created the world" (Heb 1:2); yet, at times, He would have been glad of anything, having nothing to eat:

> "On the following day, when they came from Bethany, he was hungry. And seeing in the distance a fig tree in leaf, he went to see if he could find anything on it." (Mark 11:12-13)

In this light, it is clear that God has set no mark of hatred on you; neither can you conclude a lack of love from the lack of bread. When your complaining heart asks the question, *"Was there ever any sorrow like mine,"* ask these worthy saints, and they will tell you that they were driven to as great of need as you—though they did not complain and fret as you do.

God promises to supply your needs

God has not left you in this poor condition without a promise, so you have no reason to complain or despair in it. It is a sad condition, indeed, where no promise can be found. I remember Calvin's commentary on these words in Isaiah:

> "But there will be no gloom for her who was in anguish." (Isa 9:1)

These soothing words made the darkness of the captivity not as great as the lesser incursions made by Tiglath Pileser. In the captivity, the city was destroyed, and the temple was burnt with fire—there was no comparison in the amount of suffering; and, yet, the darkness was not as oppressive. The reason, says Calvin, is that there was a certain promise made for the one, but none for the other.

It is better to be low as Hell with a promise than in Paradise without one. Even the darkness of Hell itself would be in comparison not dark at all if there were only a promise to lighten it. Now, God has left many sweet promises for the faith of His poor people to feed on in this condition, including the following verses:

"Oh, fear the Lord, you his saints,
for those who fear him have no lack!
The young lions suffer want and hunger;
but those who seek the Lord lack no good thing."
(Psalm 34:9-10)

"Behold, the eye of the Lord is on those who fear him,
on those who hope in his steadfast love,
that he may deliver their soul from death
and keep them alive in famine."
(Psalm 33:18-19)

"For the Lord God is a sun and shield;
the Lord bestows favor and honor.
No good thing does he withhold
from those who walk uprightly."
(Psalm 84:11)

"He who did not spare his own Son but gave him up for us all, how will he not also with him graciously give us all things?"
(Romans 8:32)

"When the poor and needy seek water,
and there is none,
and their tongue is parched with thirst,
I the Lord will answer them;
I the God of Israel will not forsake them."
(Isaiah 41:17)

Here, you first see their extreme needs, water representing the necessities of life. But then you see their certain relief: "I the Lord will answer them," which supposes that they cry to Him in their straits and that He hears their cry. Therefore, having these promises, why should your distrustful hearts not conclude with David:

"The Lord is my shepherd; I shall not want." (Ps 23:1)

You might object that these promises imply conditions, and if they were absolute, they would provide more comfort. However, what are those implied conditions but these: 1) that He will either supply or sanctify your desires, or 2) that you will have as much as God sees best for you. And does this trouble you? Would you have the gift whether sanctified or not—whether God sees it best for you or not? I think the appetites of saints after earthly things should not be so ravenous that they would seize greedily upon any enjoyment, not caring how they get it.

But, oh, when wants pinch and we cannot see where relief will come from, then our faith in the promise shakes; we become like Israel and cry, *He gave us water, can you also give bread?*[3] Oh, unbelieving hearts! When did His promises fail? Who ever trusted them and was ashamed? May not God reprimand you for your unreasonable infidelity? "Have I been a wilderness to [you]" (Jer 2:31).[4] In fact, can you not reprimand yourself and say with good old Polycarp, *"For many years I have served Christ and found Him to be a good master."*

God may deny what you want but not what your real *wants* call for. He will not regard the cry of your lusts, nor will He despise the cry of your faith. Though He will not indulge and humor your carnal appetites, yet He will not violate His own faithful promises. These promises are your best security for eternal life, and it is strange if they do not satisfy you for daily bread. Remind yourself of the words of the Lord, and comfort your hearts with them in the midst of all your wants. It is said of Epicurus that in his dreadful bouts with Kidney stones, he often refreshed himself by calling to mind his theories of philosophy. And Posidonius the philosopher, in a similar condition, solaced himself with discourses of moral virtue. When experiencing sharp pains, he would say, *"Oh, pain, you accomplish nothing; though you are a little troublesome, I will never confess you to be evil."* If these men could support themselves on these grounds under such grinding and wracking pains and even delude their diseases by them, how much more should the precious promises of God—and the sweet experiences that have gone along step-by-step with them—cause you to forget all your wants and comfort you in every hardship!

---

[3] Ps 78:20 "He struck the rock so that water gushed out and streams overflowed. Can he also give bread or provide meat for his people?"

[4] Jer 2:31 "And you, O generation, behold the word of the Lord. Have I been a wilderness to Israel, or a land of thick darkness? Why then do my people say, 'We are free, we will come no more to you'?"

You have more than you deserve

Even if it is bad now, it could be worse. Has God denied you the comforts of this life? He might have denied you Christ, peace, and pardon as well, and then your case would have been woeful indeed!

You know that God has done this for millions in the world. How many miserable individuals do your eyes behold every day who have no comfort in *hand*, nor any in *hope*; they are miserable here and will be so throughout eternity. It is a bitter cup and nothing with which to sweeten it—not so much as any hope that it will be better.

But it is not so with you! Though you are poor in this world, yet you are "rich in faith and heirs of the kingdom, which he has promised to those who love him" (James 2:5). Oh, learn to assess spiritual riches over and above any temporal poverty. Balance all of your present troubles with your spiritual privileges. You might do well to be downcast if God had actually denied your souls the robes of righteousness to clothe them; if you had no hidden manna to feed them; if there were no heavenly mansions to receive you; and if your souls, as well as your bodies, were left destitute. But the following words of Luther are enough to bring the thoughtful soul to rest under any outward trial. When lack began to pinch him, he bravely said, *"let us be content with our hard fare, for do we not feast with the angels on Christ, the bread of life?"* And Paul said,

> *"Blessed be the God and Father of our Lord Jesus Christ, who has blessed us in Christ with every spiritual blessing in the heavenly places." (Eph 1:3)*

Your condition could be worse

Your affliction, though great, is not the worst that God has ever used to discipline His dearly loved children in this world. And if He were to remove your current trial and replace them with those others, you would consider your present state to be very comfortable and bless God to be as you are now.

Consider this. What if God removed your present troubles, supplied all your outward wants, gave you the desires of your heart, *but* hid His face from you? What if He shot his arrows into your soul and caused the venom of them to drink of your spirit? What if He gave you over even for a few days to the buffeting of Satan and his blasphemous injections, keeping you awake for only a few nights with horrors of conscience, tossing back and forth until the dawning of the day? What if Satan then led you through the chambers of death, showed you visions of the darkness, and made his terrors set themselves against you? Then, tell me if you would not count it a precious mercy to be back again in your former needful condition but with a peaceful conscience. Would you not count bread and water with God's favor a happy state?

Oh, then! Watch out for bitter complaining. Do not say that God deals harshly with you, lest you provoke Him to convince you by your own sense and feeling that He has worse rods than yours for rebellious, grumbling children.

Suffering is short-lived

Know that if it is bad now, it will be better shortly. Oh, keep your heart with this consideration! The grain in the barrel is almost gone; well, if that is true, why should it trouble you when you are almost beyond the need and use of all these things? It is like a traveler who has spent almost all his money (only a shilling or two remaining). He says to himself, *"Even though my money is almost spent, yet my journey is almost finished too; I am close to home, and then I will have everything I need."* Or it is like a house without candles: it is a comfort to think that it is almost day when there will be no need for candles!

I am afraid, Christian, that you may have miscalculated when you think, *"My provision is almost gone, and I have a long way to travel, many years to live, and nothing to live on."* It may not be half as many as you suppose! In this be confident: if your provision is spent, either fresh supplies are coming (though you cannot see from where) or you are nearer your journey's end than you thought yourself to be.

Despondent soul, is it appropriate for men and women who are traveling up the road to that Heavenly City—and almost arrived, within a few day's journey of their Father's house, where all their needs will be supplied—to fixate in this way about a little meat, drink, or clothes that they fear they will lack on the way? It was a noble saying of the forty Martyrs,[5] when sent outside naked on a frosty night to starve to death, that with these words they comforted one another: *"winter indeed is sharp and cold, but Heaven is warm and comfortable; here, we shiver from the cold, but Abraham's bosom will make amends for all."*

You may say that you will die for want. Who has done so? When have the righteous been forsaken? If you die, your journey is ended, and you are fully supplied. However, if you are not sure of Heaven, then you have more important matters to attend to than these. Your hardship should be the least of all your worries. I do not find that souls who are perplexed and troubled about the lack of Christ, pardon of sin, or other matters of eternal significance are usually very anxious or attentive about these things. The one who seriously asks questions such as *"What should I do to be saved? How do I know my sin is pardoned?"* does not usually trouble with questions like *"What will I eat? What will I drink? How will I be clothed?"*[6]

---

[5] Flavel points out here that the forty martyrs were made famous in the *"Ecclesiastical story"*, which possibly refers to Eusebius's *Ecclesiastical History* in 325 A.D.

[6] **Matt 6:31** "Therefore do not be anxious, saying, 'What shall we eat?' or 'What shall we drink?' or 'What shall we wear?'"

God is a loving Father

Is it right that the children of such a Father should distrust His all-sufficiency or complain about any of His dispensations? Do you do well to question God's care and love at every new circumstance? Have you not been ashamed of this in the past? Has your Father not generously provided for you in former straits, which caused you to blush and resolve to never question His love and care again? And yet, will you renew your unworthy suspicions of Him again? Unfaithful child, reason this way with yourself:

> *If I perish for lack of what I think is good and necessary for me, it must be that my Father does not know my needs, or He does not have the ability to supply them, or He does not care what happens to me. Which of these will I charge Him with?*

He cannot be charged with the first; for, "your heavenly Father knows that you need them" (Matt 6:32).[7] Your Father knows what you need, and your condition is not hidden from Him. Nor can He be charged with the second; for, "the earth is the Lord's and the fullness thereof" (Ps 24:1). His name is "God Almighty" (Gen 17:1).[8] And He cannot be charged with the last:

> *"As a father shows compassion to his children, so the Lord shows compassion to those who fear him." (Ps 103:13)*

> *"The Lord is compassionate and merciful." (James 5:11)*

---

[7] **Matt 6:32** "For the Gentiles seek after all these things, and your heavenly Father knows that you need them all."

[8] **Gen 17:1** "When Abram was ninety-nine years old the Lord appeared to Abram and said to him, 'I am God Almighty; walk before me, and be blameless.'"

"Who provides for the raven its prey, when its young ones cry to God for help." (Job 38:41)

And Christ says to consider "the birds of the air" (Matt 6:26),[9] not just the birds at the door that are fed every day by hand, but the birds of the air that have no one to provide for them. Does He feed and clothe His enemies,[10] and will He forget His children? He heard the very cry of Ishmael in distress (Gen 21:17).[11] Oh, unbelieving heart! Do you still doubt? Remember Hagar and her child.

Poverty is not a sin

Remember, your poverty is not a sin—only an affliction. If it is only an affliction and has not been brought on yourself by sin, you can bear it more easily. It is hard, indeed, to bear an affliction that comes upon us as the fruit and punishment of sin. When believers experience hardship on that account, they sometimes say:

Oh! If it were only a single affliction coming from the hand of God as a trial, I could bear it; but I have brought this upon myself by sin,

---

[9] **Matt 6:32** "Look at the birds of the air: they neither sow nor reap nor gather into barns, and yet your heavenly Father feeds them. Are you not of more value than they?"

[10] **Matt 5:44** "For he makes his sun rise on the evil and on the good, and sends rain on the just and on the unjust."

[11] **Gen 21:17** "And God heard the voice of the boy, and the angel of God called to Hagar from heaven and said to her, 'What troubles you, Hagar? Fear not, for God has heard the voice of the boy where he is.'"

and it comes as a punishment of sin. It has the marks of God's displeasure on it. The internal guilt troubles and galls me more than the external hardship.

But in this case, it is not true; therefore, you have no reason to be cast down under your trial.

Although you may agree that there is no sting of guilt in your poverty, you might protest that there are yet other stings that discredit your faith by keeping you from fulfilling your responsibilities. For example, you may not be able to continue your work in the world. It is good that you have a heart to discharge every duty, yet if God prevents you by His sovereign will, it is no discredit to your faith that you do not do that which you are unable to do—as long as it is your desire, and you do what you can and ought to do. In this case, God exercises lenience and forbearance toward you (Deut 24:12-13).[12]

During these times, you may also grieve for the needs of others around you that you want to relieve but now cannot. But if you cannot do it, it ceases to be your duty. God accepts the compassionate longing of your soul to help the hungry, though you cannot open a full purse to relieve and supply them.

Lastly, although you may find this poor condition full of temptations that make your path to Heaven difficult, know that every condition in the world has its difficulties and attending temptations. If you were in a prosperous condition, you might meet with more temptations and fewer advantages than you have now. Although I admit that poverty and prosperity both have their temptations, yet I am convinced that prosperity does not have the excellent advantages that poverty has. With poverty you have the opportunity to discover the sincerity of your

---

[12] **Deut 24:12-13** "And if he is a poor man, you shall not sleep in his pledge. You shall restore to him the pledge as the sun sets, that he may sleep in his cloak and bless you. And it shall be righteousness for you before the Lord your God."

love to God; you can find your life in Him, find enough in Him, and constantly follow Him, even when all external rewards and motives fail you.

Here, I have shown you how to keep your heart from the temptations and dangers that accompany a poor and low condition in the world. When needs pinch and your heart begins to sink, then bless God for these truths to keep and heal it.

Chapter 8

A Season of Duty

The sixth season for exercising this diligence in keeping the heart is a season of spiritual duties. When you draw near to God in public, private, or secret duties, then it is time to look after the heart; for these times are the most apt to uncover its vanity. How often does the poor soul cry out:

Oh, Lord how I long to serve You, but my distracted thoughts will not let me; I came to open my heart to You and to delight my soul in communion with You, but my corruptions have set upon me. Lord, run off these vain thoughts, and do not allow them to prostitute my soul, which is wedded to You, before Your eyes.

How can our hearts be kept from such distracting thoughts when we serve God? There are two distinct kinds of distractions or wanderings of the heart in spiritual duties.

The first type of heart-wandering is voluntary and habitual—"a generation whose heart was not steadfast, whose spirit was not faithful to God" (Ps 78:8).[1] This is the case of formalists, and it is caused by the lack of a holy desire and inclination toward the heart of God. Their hearts are under the power of their lusts; therefore, it is no wonder that they go after their lusts, even when they are engaged in holy things (Ezek 33:31).[2]

The second type of distraction is involuntary and lamented:

"So I find it to be a law that when I want to do right, evil lies close at hand. Wretched man that I am!" (Rom 7:21,24)

This does not proceed from the lack of a holy desire or aim, but from the weakness and imperfection of grace. And in this case, the soul may raise a complaint against its own corruptions that echoes Abijah's complaint against Jeroboam that he "rebelled against his lord" and gathered "worthless scoundrels" around him in the revolt (2 Chron 13:6-7).[3] Grace has a dominion, but lusts are mutinous and seditious from the outset. But it is not my intent to show you how these distractions come into the heart but, rather, to get and keep them out of the heart. To this end, consider the following ten practices.

---

[1] **Ps 78:8** "And that they should not be like their fathers, a stubborn and rebellious generation, a generation whose heart was not steadfast, whose spirit was not faithful to God."

[2] **Ezek 33:31** "And they come to you as people come, and they sit before you as my people, and they hear what you say but they will not do it; for with lustful talk in their mouths they act; their heart is set on their gain."

[3] **2 Chron 13:6-7** "Yet Jeroboam the son of Nebat, a servant of Solomon the son of David, rose up and rebelled against his lord, and certain worthless scoundrels gathered about him and defied Rehoboam the son of Solomon, when Rehoboam was young and irresolute and could not withstand them."

Quiet your heart before God

Separate yourself from all earthly tasks, and set apart some time for solemn preparation to meet God in your spiritual duties; you cannot come reeking hot out of the world into God's presence without finding a tang of the world in your duties. Your heart comes to the feet of God, but it has only minutes earlier been plunged into the world; it is like the sea after a storm, whose unsettled muddy waters continue to churn, even though the winds have calmed and the storm is over. Your heart must have some time to settle. Few musicians can take down a guitar or violin and immediately start playing without some time to tune it; and there are few Christians who can immediately say with the psalmist, "my heart is steadfast, O God, my heart is steadfast!" (Ps 57:7). Oh, when you go to God in any duty, take your heart aside and say:

Oh, my soul! I am now applying myself to the greatest work that an individual could ever do; I am going into the awesome presence of God to a task with eternal significance. Oh, my soul! Leave worldly cares now; be composed, watchful, and serious. This is no common work—it is God-work, soul-work, and eternity-work. I am now going forth bearing seed that will bring forth fruit to life or death in the world to come.

In this way, pause awhile to look upon your sins, desires, and troubles; steep your thoughts in these before you address yourself to your spiritual duties. David first meditated and then spoke with his tongue:

"My heart became hot within me.
As I mused, the fire burned;
then I spoke with my tongue." (Ps 39:3-4)

109

"My heart overflows with a pleasing theme;
I address my verses to the king;
my tongue is like the pen of a ready scribe." (Ps 45:1)

Guard against distractions

Having composed your heart in meditation, immediately set a guard on your senses. How often are poor Christians in danger of losing the eyes of their mind by those of the body? For this reason, Job "made a covenant with [his] eyes" (Job 31:1). And David prayed:

"Turn my eyes from looking at worthless things;
and give me life in your ways." (Ps 119:37)

This may explain that mystical Arabian proverb that recommends to *"shut the windows that the house may be light."* It would be great if at the outset of any service to God if you could say (as a holy one once did when he came off from his duty): *"Be shut my eyes; be shut! For it is impossible that you should ever see such beauty and glory in any creature as I have now seen in God."* It is necessary to avoid all opportunities for external distractions, for you will be sure to meet with enough from within. An intent spirit locks up the eye and ear against the flesh during any service to God. When Marcellus entered the gates of Syracuse, Archimedes was so intent on his mathematical scheme that he took no notice of the soldiers when they entered into his study with their swords drawn. A fervent heart cannot be a vagrant heart.

Pray for sanctified thoughts

Plead for God to sanctify your imagination. It is said that an active imagination, however much it is extolled by others, is a great snare to the soul (unless it works in conjunction with sound reasoning and a sanctified heart). The imagination is that power of the soul that is placed between the senses and the understanding; it is that which first stirs within the soul and, by its motion, stirs other powers. It is typically the place where thoughts are first forged and framed, and as the imagination goes, so they go; if imaginations are not first cast down, it is impossible that every thought of the heart should be brought into obedience to Christ (2 Cor 10:5).[4] Our imagination is naturally the wildest and most untamable power in the soul. Many Christians have much to work on here.

And, truly, the more spiritual the heart, the more troubled it is about its vanity and wildness. Oh, what a sad thing it is that your nobler soul must follow up and down after a vain roving fancy. You find yourself called away from the presence of God and sweet communion with Him to pursue fancies that would have alarmed you before! It is like a beggar riding horseback with a prince running after him on foot.

Beg earnestly to God that the power of sanctification may come upon such thoughts at once. Some Christians have attained such a high degree of sanctification of their thoughts that they have had much sweetness left upon their hearts by the spiritual workings of it in the night. When your imagination is more sanctified, your thoughts will be more orderly and fixed.

Respect the holy presence of God

If you want to keep your heart from these frivolous excursions, in faith remember that you are in the holy and awesome presence of God in your duties. If the presence of a serious man will compose you to seriousness, how much more should the presence of a holy God? Do

[4] **2 Cor 10:5** "We destroy arguments and every lofty opinion raised against the knowledge of God, and take every thought captive to obey Christ."

you think that your soul would be so brash and light if you sensed the gaze of a divine eye on it? Remember the place where you are is the place at His feet (Isa 60:13).[5] Act in faith on the omniscience of God.

"And all the churches will know that I am he who searches mind and heart, and I will give to each of you according to your works." (Rev 2:23)

"And no creature is hidden from his sight, but all are naked and exposed to the eyes of him to whom we must give account." (Heb 4:13)

Realize how infinitely holy He is; consider how serious and composed Isaiah became at the sight of God in His holiness (Isa 6:5).[6] Also work to impress upon your heart a right understanding of the greatness of God, such as Abraham had:

"Behold, I have undertaken to speak to the Lord, I who am but dust and ashes." (Gen 18:27)

And, lastly, remember the jealousy of God and how concerned He is over His worship:

[5] **Isa 60:13** "The glory of Lebanon shall come to you, the cypress, the plane, and the pine, to beautify the place of my sanctuary, and I will make the place of my feet glorious."

[6] **Isa 6:5** "And I said: 'Woe is me! For I am lost; for I am a man of unclean lips, and I dwell in the midst of a people of unclean lips; for my eyes have seen the King, the Lord of hosts!'"

"This is what the Lord has said: 'Among those who are near me I will be sanctified, and before all the people I will be glorified.'"
(Lev 10:3)

Bernard says that a man who is praying should compose himself as if he were entering into the court of Heaven and seeing the Lord upon His throne surrounded with ten thousand of His angels and with saints ministering to Him. When you come from an act of worship in which your heart has been distracted and wandering, you may say, *"Surely, God was in this place, and I did not know it."* What if all the foolish vanities that have passed through your heart in prayer were written out and interlined with your petitions? Would you have the gall to present it to God? If your tongue simply uttered all the thoughts of your heart in prayer, would others not abhor you? But your thoughts are vocal to God (Ps 139:2).[7] If you were petitioning the king for your life, would he not be provoked to see you playing with your shoestrings or catching every fly that lands on your clothes while you were speaking to him about such serious matters? Oh, think soberly upon this scripture:

"God [is] greatly to be feared in the council of the holy ones, and awesome above all who are around him." (Ps 89:7)

See yourself standing before God in this way, and your vain heart will quickly be reduced to a more serious frame.

---

[7] **Ps 139:2** "You know when I sit down and when I rise up; you discern my thoughts from afar."

Pray consistently

Maintain a praying frame of heart between formal spiritual duties. What is the reason that our hearts are so dull, careless, and wandering when we come to pray? Is it not due to such long intermissions in our communion with God that our hearts have gotten out of a praying frame? If that spiritual warmth—those holy impressions we carry from God in one duty—were only preserved to kindle another duty, it would be a marvelous advantage to keep our hearts intent and serious toward God.

To this purpose, those short prayers between stated and solemn duties can be put to most sweet and excellent use. By these, one duty is, in a sense, linked to another, and so the soul is wrapped up in a chain of duties. The Christian who regularly shoots up many of these darts of prayer seldom misses the mark when it comes to formal duties. It is an excellent compliment that Christ bestows on the spouse: "Your lips drip nectar, my bride" (Song 4:11). While the honeycomb drops only occasionally, it always hangs full of sweet drops ready to fall; if our prayers were more, our lamentations would be fewer.

Cultivate love for God

Endeavor to engage and raise your affections to God in your spiritual duties if you desire to be cured of your distractions. Damp eyes and melted hearts are seldom troubled as others are on this account. When the soul is intent on any work, it gathers in its strength and bends all its thoughts intently around it. The affections command the thoughts to go after them; however, deadness causes distraction, and distraction increases deadness. If you could only look upon your spiritual duties as the galleries in which you walk and commune with God—a place where your soul may be filled with those ravishing and matchless delights that are in His presence—your soul would not want to stir from there.

It is with the heart in duty as it is with those who dig for gold; they try here and, finding none, try there. They go from place to place until, at last, they hit upon a rich vein, and there they stay. If your heart could but once hit a rich vein in duty, it would dwell and abide there with delight and constancy.

> "Oh how I love your law!
> It is my meditation all the day." (Ps 119:97)

The soul could dwell both day and night on its knees once its delights, loves, and desires are engaged. What is the reason your heart is so wandering, especially in secret duties? Why are you ready to be gone almost as soon as you have come into the presence of God? It is because your affections are not engaged.

Cry to God for help

Therefore, when vain thoughts assault your heart in your spiritual duties, mourn over the matter to God, and call for assistance from Heaven. When a messenger of Satan harassed Paul with wicked injections, as is supposed, he went to God and mourned over the matter before Him (2 Cor 12:8).[8] Never consider wandering thoughts in worship to be a small matter; follow every vain thought with a deep sigh, and turn to God with such words as these:

---

[8] **2 Cor 12:8** "Three times I pleaded with the Lord about this, that it should leave me."

Lord, I came here to speak with You, and now a busy devil and a vain heart have conspired together to set upon me. Oh, my God, what a heart I have! Will I never come to You without distraction? When will I enjoy an hour of free communion with You? Help me this once, my God! Display Your glory before my eyes, and my heart will quickly be restored. You know I came here to enjoy You, and will I leave without You? See how the heart of Your poor child works toward You and strives to get nearer to You but cannot! My heart has run aground. "Awake, O north wind, and come, O south wind!"[9] Send a fresh gale now from Your Spirit to set my affections afloat!

If you could affectionately mourn your distractions to God in this way, you might obtain help and deliverance from them. He would say to Satan and your arrogant lusts as King Ahasuerus said to Haman:

"Will he even assault the queen in my presence?" (Est 7:8). What are these thoughts that set upon My child in My presence?

See the benefits of a focused heart

Consider that the success and sweetness of your duties are very much dependent on keeping your heart close with God while performing them. These two things—the success and sweetness of duties—are as dear to a Christian as two eyes; and both of these are sure to be lost if the heart is lost in duty.

"Surely God does not hear an empty cry,
nor does the Almighty regard it." (Job 35:13)

---

[9] Song 4:16

But the following promise is made to a heart that is engaged:

"You will seek me and find me,
when you seek me with all your heart." (Jer 29:13)

So, when you find your heart under the power of deadness and distraction, say to your soul:

Soul, see what I lose by a careless heart now! My praying times are the finest parts and the golden moments of all my time. If I could only raise up this heart with God, I might now obtain such mercies that would be worthy of a song for all eternity.

Test yourself

Look on it as a great discovery of the sincerity or hypocrisy of your heart as to whether you find yourself careful or careless in this matter. Nothing will alarm an upright heart more than this:

What, will I give ground to a customary wandering of my heart from God? Will the spot of the hypocrite appear upon my soul? Others can drudge on in their duties, never regarding the frames of their hearts (Ezek 33:31-32);[10] but will I do so? When men come into the inner courts and the King is not there, they bow to the empty chair. Oh, never let me be satisfied with empty duties! Never let me take

---

[10] **Ezek 33:31-32** "And they come to you as people come, and they sit before you as my people, and they hear what you say but they will not do it; for with lustful talk in their mouths they act; their heart is set on their gain. And behold, you are to them like one who sings lustful songs with a beautiful voice and plays well on an instrument, for they hear what you say, but they will not do it."

my leave of a duty until "my eyes have seen the King, the Lord of hosts!"[11]

Serve with eternity in mind

Lastly, you will find that it is easier to keep your heart with God in your spiritual service when you consider the influence they have on your eternal destiny. This is a time for planting seed; what you sow in your duties in this world, you should look to reap the fruit of in the next.

> *"Do not be deceived: God is not mocked, for whatever one sows, that will he also reap. For the one who sows to his own flesh will from the flesh reap corruption, but the one who sows to the Spirit will from the Spirit reap eternal life." (Gal 6:7-8)*

Oh, answer seriously: would you be willing to reap the fruit of vanity in the world to come? When your thoughts are roving to the ends of the earth during worship and you scarcely know what you are doing, should you not say:

> *Now, Lord, I am sowing to the Spirit. Now, I am providing and laying up for eternity. Now, I am seeking for glory, honor, and immortality. Now, I am striving to enter in at the narrow gate, and I am taking the Kingdom of Heaven by a holy violence.*

---

[11] **Isa 6:5** "And I said: 'Woe is me! For I am lost; for I am a man of unclean lips, and I dwell in the midst of a people of unclean lips; for my eyes have seen the King, the Lord of hosts!'"

Oh, such considerations as this should cause the multitudes of vain thoughts that press in upon your heart in duty to fly off in seven directions. In this way, I have shown you how to keep your hearts during times of spiritual duties.

Chapter 9

A Season of Wrongs

The seventh season that calls for more diligence to keep the heart is when we are injured or abused by others. The depravity and corruption of mankind in their collapsed state is such that they have become a wolf or a tiger to each other. They are, as the prophet complains, "like the fish of the sea, like crawling things that have no ruler" (Hab 1:14). And as wicked men are cruel and oppressive to one another, so they conspire together to abuse and wrong the people of God: "The wicked swallows up the man more righteous than he" (v. 13).

Now, when we are abused and wronged in this way, it is hard to keep the heart from motives of revenge but, instead, meekly and quietly commit our cause to Him who judges righteously. And it is difficult to exercise no other emotion but pity toward those who abuse us. Surely, the spirit within us longs for revenge, but it must not be so. We have excellent aids in the Gospel to sweeten our embittered spirits and to calm our hearts from such sinful actions against our enemies.

How can we keep our hearts from seeking revenge when others greatly injure and abuse us? The Gospel allows us the freedom to vindicate our innocence and to assert our rights, but we are not permitted to vent our anger and take God's rightful place. Therefore, when you find your heart is beginning to burn with a desire for revenge, immediately apply the following remedies.

Remember God's prohibition against revenge

Impress upon your heart the severe prohibitions against revenge by the Law of God. Remember that no matter how pleasing and luscious revenge appears to our fallen appetites, it is forbidden fruit. Nature says that revenge is sweet, but God says the effects will be bitter. And He has plainly forbidden this flesh-pleasing sin in many scriptures:

> *"Do not say, 'I will repay evil';*
> *wait for the Lord, and he will deliver you." (Prov 20:22)*

> *"Do not say, 'I will do to him as he has done to me;*
> *I will pay the man back for what he has done.'" (Prov 24:29)*

> *"Repay no one evil for evil, but give thought to do what is honorable*
> *in the sight of all. Beloved, never avenge yourselves, but leave it to*
> *the wrath of God, for it is written, 'Vengeance is mine, I will repay,*
> *says the Lord.'" (Rom 12:17,19)*

And that is not all:

> *"If your enemy is hungry, give him bread to eat,*
> *and if he is thirsty, give him water to drink." (Prov 25:21)*

The phrase, "give him bread to eat," as commentators observe, signifies to feed him cheerfully and tenderly, as birds do for their young ones.

Scripture is a great friend to the peace and tranquility of human society, which can never be preserved if revenge is not eliminated. It has been argued that Christianity is supernatural and pure because it forbids revenge which is so sweet to nature; and it is surely a thousand pities if such an argument should be lost.

Therefore, awe your hearts with the authority of God in these scriptures. And when your carnal reason says, *"My enemies deserve to be hated,"* let your conscience reply:

> *But does God deserve to be disobeyed? My enemy has done this and that, and so he has wronged me; but what has God done that I should wrong Him? If my enemy dares to be so bold as to break the peace, will I be so wicked as to break the precept? If he does not fear to wrong me, will I not fear to wrong God?*

Oh, let the fear of God's commands repress such sinful responses.

Look at Christ's example

Set the most eminent patterns of meekness and forgiveness before your eyes so that your soul may fall in love with it. This is the way to cut off the most common pleas of the flesh for revenge, such as "no man would bear such an affront" (yes, others have borne as bad and worse); or "I will be reckoned a coward and fool if I pass this by" (no matter, as long as you follow the example of the wisest and holiest men). And no one has ever suffered more or experienced greater abuse from men than Christ, and no one has borne it more peaceably and forgivingly.

> *"He was oppressed, and he was afflicted,*
> *yet he opened not his mouth;*
> *like a lamb that is led to the slaughter,*
> *and like a sheep that before its shearers is silent,*
> *so he opened not his mouth." (Isa 53:7)*

The apostle sets this pattern before you for your imitation:

"For to this you have been called, because Christ also suffered for you, leaving you an example, so that you might follow in his steps. He committed no sin, neither was deceit found in his mouth. When he was reviled, he did not revile in return; when he suffered, he did not threaten, but continued entrusting himself to him who judges justly." (1 Pet 2:21-23)

To have a humble, forgiving spirit is Christ-like and God-like:

"But I say to you, Love your enemies and pray for those who persecute you, so that you may be sons of your Father who is in heaven. For he makes his sun rise on the evil and on the good, and sends rain on the just and on the unjust." (Matt 5:45)

Also, consider how eminently this Spirit of Christ rested on His Apostles. Never were there men on the earth with such excellency of Spirit, and none were ever abused more or handled their abuses better.

"When reviled, we bless; when persecuted, we endure; when slandered, we entreat." (1 Cor 4:12-13)

Calvin was a spirited man, yet he had attained such a degree of this Christ-like forgiveness that when Luther had spoken scornfully of him, the good man said no more than this, "Although he should call me a devil, yet I will acknowledge him to be an eminent servant of Jesus Christ."

I have often heard the following report of holy Mr. Dod. A man who was enraged at his convicting doctrine picked a quarrel with him and then struck him on the face, knocking out two of his teeth. This meek servant of Christ spat out the teeth and blood into his hand and said, "see here, you have knocked out two of my teeth—and that without any just provocation; but if it might do your soul good, I would give you leave to dash out all the rest."

Here is the excellence of a Christian's spirit above all the attainments of moral heathens: though they were excellent at many other things, yet they could never attain this forgiving spirit. Tully said that it was the first office of justice to hurt no one unless first provoked by an injury, to which Lactantius responded, "What a wonderful sentence that the orator spoiled by adding those last two words!" Therefore, strive for this excellence of Spirit, which is the proper mindset for Christians. Do this singular thing that others cannot do, and then you will have a testimony in their consciences. When Moses outdid the magicians, they were forced to confess the finger of God in his actions (Ex 8:19).[1]

Consider the offender

Carefully consider the quality of the one who has wronged you: they are either a good or a wicked person. If the offender is good at heart, then there is a light and tenderness of conscience that might eventually bring about a conviction for the evil that has been done to you. Also, Christ has forgiven them for even greater injuries, so why shouldn't you? Won't Christ reproach them with any of those wrongs done to Him, while forgiving them completely? Will you then grab them by the throat for some petty abuse that has been done to you?

On the other hand, what if a wicked person injures you? If so, you truly have more reason to exercise pity than revenge—and that upon a

---

[1] **Ex 8:19** "Then the magicians said to Pharaoh, 'This is the finger of God.' But Pharaoh's heart was hardened, and he would not listen to them, as the Lord had said."

double account. First, they are not in their right mind, and so is every unconverted sinner (Luke 15:17).[2] If you went to a mental institution and heard one rail at you, another mock you, and a third threaten you, would you then say, *"I will be revenged upon them!"*? No, you would instead go away pitying them, saying *"Alas, poor creatures, they are out of their minds and do not know what they are saying."* Second, there is a day coming when, if they do not repent, they will have more misery than you can find in your heart to wish on them. God's vengeance does not sleep. This will shortly fall on them, and is that not enough? Is there not an eternity of misery coming? If they do not repent, this must be a portion of their punishment, and if they ever do repent, they will be ready to make you reparations.

See victory in forgiveness

Keep your heart with this consideration: by vengeance, you can satisfy a lust; but by forgiveness, you will conquer a lust. Suppose by revenge you could destroy one enemy; I will show you how by forgiving you can conquer three: your own lusts, the Devil's temptation, and your enemy's heart. And is this not a more glorious conquest? By revenge, you can overcome your enemy, yet, as Bernard says, it is an unhappy victory when in the process of overcoming another person, you are overcome by your own corruptions. But forgiveness offers a glorious conquest indeed. Consider the honorable victory that David obtained in this way over Saul:

> *"As soon as David had finished speaking these words to Saul, Saul said, 'Is this your voice, my son David?' And Saul lifted up his voice*

---

[2] **Luke 15:17** "But when he came to himself, he said, 'How many of my father's hired servants have more than enough bread, but I perish here with hunger!'"

and wept. He said to David, 'You are more righteous than I, for you have repaid me good, whereas I have repaid you evil.'"
(1 Sam 24:16-17)

It is a very disingenuous nature, indeed, who is not affected by meekness and forgiveness; this fire can melt the stoniest heart. This is the sense of the proverb:

"If your enemy is hungry, give him bread to eat,
and if he is thirsty, give him water to drink,
for you will heap burning coals on his head,
and the Lord will reward you." (Prov 25:21)

For some, it will be a sin-punishing fire, but others will experience a heart-melting fire. To be sure, it will either melt their heart or aggravate their misery. Augustine thinks that Stephen's prayer for his enemies was a significant means of Paul's conversion.[3]

Find the good in your injury

Seriously pose this question to your heart: *have you or have you not received any good by the wrong and injuries that have been done to you?* If they have done you no good, turn your thoughts of revenge on yourself:

Oh, that I should have such a bad heart than I can find no good in my troubles. Oh, that my spirit is so unlike Christ's! The patience and meekness of other Christians have turned all the injuries thrown at them into precious stones; the spirits of others have been

---

[3] See Stephen's speech and stoning in the presence of Saul in Acts 7.

raised to bless God when they have been loaded with the reproaches of the world. They have bound them as an ornament around their necks.

Luther said that he could even be proud that he had a bad name among wicked men. For the same reason, Jerome sweetly said that he thanked God that he was worthy to be hated by the world. In this way, their hearts were provoked by injuries to magnify God and bless Him for them. If this is not the case for you, do you not have cause to be filled with self-reproach?

If you have gotten any good by them; if the reproaches and wrongs you have received have made you search your heart more and watch your ways more carefully; or if their wrongs toward you have made you see how you have wronged God, then let me say for them, as Paul did for himself, pray forgive them this wrong.

Can you not find it in your heart to forgive someone who has been the instrument of so much good to you? Though they meant it for evil, God has turned it to good.[4] You have no more reason to rage against the instrument than a man who received a wound from an enemy which only drained an abscess that otherwise would have killed him.

Remember God's sovereignty

One excellent way to keep your heart from revenge is to look up and see the first cause by which all your troubles are ordered. This will quickly calm and humble your spirit.

Never did a wicked tongue try the patience of a saint more than when David was tried by that railing Shimei; yet David's spirit was not at all poisoned with revenge. Though Shimei continued cursing and

---

[4] A reference to Joseph's words to his brothers in Genesis 50:15-21.

casting stones at him all along the way and though Abishai offered David the head of that enemy if he pleased, the king said:

> *"What have I to do with you, you sons of Zeruiah? If he is cursing because the Lord has said to him, 'Curse David,' who then shall say, 'Why have you done so?'" (2 Sam 20:10)*

It may be that God used Shimei as His rod to lash David because David by his sin made His enemies to blaspheme Him. And should David be angry with the rod? How irrational would that be?

This also was what quieted Job. He does not rail and vow revenge upon the Chaldeans and Sabeans; rather, he sees God as the orchestrator of those troubles, and he is quiet:

> *"And he said, 'Naked I came from my mother's womb, and naked shall I return. The Lord gave, and the Lord has taken away; blessed be the name of the Lord.'" (Job 1:21)*

But you might object that "to subvert a man in his cause, the Lord approveth not" (Lam 3:36, KJV). True, it does not fall under His approving will, yet it does belong to His permitting will. And this is a great argument for our quiet submission. In fact, He not only permits but orders all our troubles. If we saw more of our holy God, we would show less of a corrupt nature in our trials.

Reflect on God's mercies

Consider how you daily wrong God, and you will not be so easily inflamed with revenge against others who have wronged you. You are daily grieving and wronging God, and yet He bears, forgives, and refrains from taking vengeance on you. So will you be so quick to avenge yourself on others? We see a sharp and terrible rebuke of this in Matthew:

> *"Then his master summoned him and said to him, 'You wicked servant! I forgave you all that debt because you pleaded with me. And should not you have had mercy on your fellow servant, as I had mercy on you?'" (Matt 18:32-33)*

None should be more filled with depths of pity, forbearance, and mercy to those who have wronged them, as those who have experienced the riches of mercy for themselves. I think the mercies of God toward us should melt our very hearts into mercies for others. It is impossible that we can be *cruel* to others except that we forget how *kind* Christ has been to us. Those that have found mercy should show mercy. And if kindness cannot motivate us, I think fear should:

> *"But if you do not forgive others their trespasses, neither will your Father forgive your trespasses." (Matt 6:15)*

Know that the Lord will avenge

Lastly, let the consideration of the Day of the Lord, which draws near, restrain your heart from preempting it by acts of revenge. Why are you quick? Is the Lord not at hand to avenge all his abused servants?

> *"Be patient, therefore, brothers, until the coming of the Lord. See how the farmer waits for the precious fruit of the earth, being patient about it, until it receives the early and the late rains. You also, be patient. Establish your hearts, for the coming of the Lord is at hand. Do not grumble against one another, brothers, so that you may not be judged; behold, the Judge is standing at the door." (James 5:7-9)*

This passage provides three arguments against revenge: the Lord's near approach, the example of the farmer's patience, and the danger we draw on ourselves by preempting God's judgment; "Vengeance is mine...says the Lord" (Rom 12:19).[5] He will distribute justice more equally and impartially than you can. Those who know they have a God to vindicate them will not sin by avenging their own wrongs.

However, you might object that our nature is not able to bear such abuses. If you resolve to consult only the natural self in such cases and go no further than what that will enable you to do, then do not pretend to be a Christian. Christians must do singular and supernatural things.

Or you could fear that if you allow such abuses that you will be considered a fool, and everyone will trample on you. You may be reckoned so among fools, but God and good men will credit it to you as wisdom and the excellence of your spirit. It must be a vile person indeed who will trample upon a humble and forgiving Christian.

In these ways, learn to keep your hearts from revenge under all provocations.

---

[5] **Rom 12:19** "Beloved, never avenge yourselves, but leave it to the wrath of God, for it is written, 'Vengeance is mine, I will repay, says the Lord.'"

Chapter 10

A Season of Anger

The next season in which we are in danger of losing our hearts is when we meet with great crosses and provocations. Then sinful passions are apt to corrupt the heart. It is the fault of many good Christians to be quick-tempered when provoked. Although they dare not allow anger to develop into malice—for that would be a sign of wickedness—yet they are very quick to sudden anger, which is a sign of weakness.

On the life of Calvin, Beza observed that he was of a strong and hasty spirit. Beza also wrote of the great Cameron that his anger was easily stirred toward his closest friends, but then he would easily depose it and acknowledge his weakness. Sadly, when we experience provocations and trials of our patience, we sometimes lose control of our spirits. The eighth question then is this: *how can our hearts be kept humble and patient under great crosses and provocations?*

There are three sorts of anger: natural, holy, and sinful anger. Natural anger is nothing but the feeling of instinctive irritation toward an offensive object, and this is not inherently a sin. These are the precursors to passion rather than passion; they are responses rather than the sins of nature, as Jerome calls them. The reason, says Plutarch, is what is driving them. The soul is like a chariot, and the horses that draw it forward are the passionate and quick-tempered appetites; when these are rightly managed by reason, they are not only lawful but very useful to the soul. God does not want us to be mindless and unfeeling, though he does want us to be humble and patient.

"Be angry and do not sin; do not let the sun go down on your anger."
(Eph 4:26)

In this verse, God allows the natural response but forbids the sinful excess.

Holy anger is a pure flame, which is kindled by a heavenly spark of love to God. In Scripture, it is called zeal, which is (as one has said) the dagger that love draws in God's quarrel. Such was Lot's anger against the Sodomites or Moses's anger against the idolatrous Israelites.[1] When Servetus condemned Zwinglius for his harshness, he answered, "In other cases, I will be mild, but in the cause of Christ, not so." Here, that which the World calls moderation and mildness is, in God's account, stupidity and cowardness. These are not what I am now persuading you to keep your hearts against.

However, sinful anger is the thing that endangers you. Anger becomes sinful when it is either causeless (Matt 5:22)[2] or excessive. When we exceed the appropriate response of the natural cause, in measure or duration, it is a sin and a matter of shame before God. Now, consider the following ways to keep your heart from sinful anger when provoked.

---

[1] Referring to the golden calf. See Exodus 32.

[2] **Matt 5:22** "But I say to you that everyone who is angry with his brother will be liable to judgment; whoever insults his brother will be liable to the council; and whoever says, 'You fool!' will be liable to the hell of fire."

Humble yourself

If you achieve low and humble thoughts of yourself, then you will have meek spirits and a peaceful disposition toward others. The humble man is ever the patient man, but a lofty man will be an irritable spirit. Pride is the root of passion; inflated balloons will not lie close together, but prick them, and you can pack a thousand in a small room.

"By insolence comes nothing but strife." (Prov 13:10)

When we overrate ourselves, then we think we are unworthily treated by others, and that provokes us. And here, by the way, note one of the greatest benefits for acquainting yourself with your own heart: it enables you to humble and calm your spirits. Christian, I think that you should know so much of your sin that it is impossible that anyone could lay you lower or have baser thoughts of you than you have of yourself. Some translate the original text of Habakkuk 2:5 as, "the proud man is like one who abuses wine,"[3] and drunks know that they are quarrelsome. Oh, gain more humility, and that will bring you more peace.

Spend time with God

Regularly refresh your spirit by communing with God, and you will not easily be embittered with wrath toward others. A quiet conscience never produced a disquieted conversation. The peace of God rules in the heart as a judge who rules over conflict, which is the implication of Colossians 3:15:

---

[3] **Hab 2:5** "Moreover, wine is a traitor, an arrogant man who is never at rest. His greed is as wide as Sheol; like death he has never enough. He gathers for himself all nations and collects as his own all peoples."

"And let the peace of Christ rule in your hearts, to which indeed you were called in one body. And be thankful." (Col 3:15)

Wrath and strife are completely opposite to the frame and temperament of a spiritual heart; they are inconsistent with the delight and contentment of that dove-like Spirit, which loves a calm and quiet breast. The soul that feeds upon the sweet communion of the Spirit says:

Oh, shall the sparks of provocations now light my passions and raise such a smoke in my soul that will offend and drive away the Comforter from me?

This is such an effective remedy against sinful anger that I almost dare quick-tempered Christians to make forbearance a sign of communion with God. If you see such Christians quiet and calm under provocations, it is very likely that their souls are feeding upon such sweetness in God that they are loath to leave. On the other hand, if you find Christians who are turbulent and loud, doubtless they are not well within; their spirits are like a bone out of joint that cannot move without pain and trouble.

Recognize the evil of sinful anger

It is important to rightly understand the evil nature and effects of sinful anger. Anger is said to be a temporary insanity, a fever of the soul, and an eclipse of reason. The effects of it are also very sad.

First, it "grieves the Holy Spirit of God," (Eph 4:30) banishing Him from the breast of the one who rages and fumes. God is the God of peace; the presence and comforts of God are only enjoyed in a calm. It is a golden note you receive, which was seen in the previously cited verse (Col 3:15).[4] God does not usually bless us with a peaceful conscience if we do not make a practice of peace.

Second, it gives advantages to the devil:

"Be angry and do not sin; do not let the sun go down on your anger, and give no opportunity to the devil." (Eph 4:26-27)

Satan is an angry and discontented spirit, who finds no rest except in restless hearts. He lives like the salamander in the fires of contention; he rouses himself when the spirits are in a commotion. Sometimes he fills the heart with thoughts of revenge. At other times, he fills the lips and inflames the tongue with indecent language. Even the meek Moses sometimes spoke unadvisedly with his lips.

Third, it untunes the spirit for duty. For this reason, the apostle discourages husbands and wives from jarring arguments and demeanors, that their prayers should not be hindered (1 Pet 3:7).[5] All acts of worship must be suitable to the object of worship, and God is the God of peace and love.

Lastly, it disparages the Christian faith. How Plato and Pythagoras would shame us if they were still living. Christ was a lamb for His meekness, and should His followers be like lions? Oh, keep your hearts, or you will at once lose not only your own peace, but the credibility of the Gospel.

---

[4] **Col 3:15** "And let the peace of Christ rule in your hearts, to which indeed you were called in one body. And be thankful."

[5] **1 Pet 3:7** "Likewise, husbands, live with your wives in an understanding way, showing honor to the woman as the weaker vessel, since they are heirs with you of the grace of life, so that your prayers may not be hindered."

Know the joys of victory over sin

Consider how sweet it is when you conquer your own corruptions and carry away the spoil!

"Whoever is slow to anger is better than the mighty,
and he who rules his spirit than he who takes a city." (Prov 16:32)

Is there any contentment in venting your anger? How much more contentment is there in killing it? When you lie down at night (or on your death bed) and review your life, how comforting it will then be to reflect on the conquests you have achieved by the fear of the Lord over the evil tendencies of your own heart! It was a memorable saying of Emperor Valentinian when he came to die: "Among all my conquests, there is only one that now comforts me: I have overcome my worst enemy—my own heart."

Look at past examples of humility

Shame yourself by considering the most eminent and excellent patterns of humility. Above all, compare your spirit with the Spirit of Christ.

"Take my yoke upon you, and learn from me, for I am gentle and
lowly in heart, and you will find rest for your souls." (Matt 11:29)

Christ was gentle and lowly, so how can you be proud and passionate? This was also the commendation of Moses:

"Now the man Moses was very meek, more than all people who
were on the face of the earth." (Num 12:3)

It was said of Calvin and Ursinus that they were both quick-tempered, but they had so learned the meekness of Christ as to not utter one word under the greatest and most shameful provocations.

We can also be ashamed when we read the great stories of past philosophers and scholars, heathens who never had the advantages we now enjoy. Whatever feuds Pythagoreans had among themselves during the day, they would silence by sending each other this message: *"The sun is almost set."* And Plato would say to his scholar: *"I would beat you if I were not angry."* When I read of how Lycurgus showed such leniency and tenderness to an insolent man who had struck out one of his eyes, I am ashamed to see how much Christians are outshot by heathens. With only mere moral arguments and precepts, they humbled their spirits and conquered their passions. The dim light of nature taught Seneca to say that anger will hurt a man more than the offense; for there is a certain bound in the offense, but you do not know how far your anger will carry you. It is a shame that these men, who were so far behind us in truth and advantages, should so far outstrip us in meekness and patience.

Avoid occasions of anger

He who will not hear the bell must not pull the rope. "a harsh word stirs up anger" (Prov 15:1).[6] Do not only pray and resolve against sinful anger, but get as far as you can out of the way of it. It is true spiritual valor to run as fast and as far as you can go away from sin. If you could only avoid anger in its first rise, there is no great reason to fear it later; for it is not with this sin as it is with other sins. Other sins grow to their full strength by degrees with their first movements being the weakest. But the sin of anger is born in its full strength, and it is strongest at first. Withstand it then, and it will fall before you.

---

[6] **Prov 15:1** "A soft answer turns away wrath, but a harsh word stirs up anger."

In these ways, learn to keep your hearts when provocations arise.

Chapter 11

A Season of Temptation

The ninth season in which we must exercise the greatest diligence is during the critical hour of temptation—a time when Satan makes close siege on the royal fort of a Christian's heart. We are often surprised due to a lack of watchfulness. To keep your heart at these times is no less a mercy than a duty, and few Christians are well trained to detect the lies and arguments that Satan uses to draw them into sin so as to safely come away from those encounters. Consider the words of our Lord:

> *"Watch and pray that you may not enter into temptation. The spirit indeed is willing, but the flesh is weak." (Mark 14:38)*

Even the eminent David and the wise Solomon were stung for their carelessness during times of temptation. This leads to the next question: *how can we keep our hearts from yielding to temptations when we are strongly solicited by the Devil to sin*? Now, there are six special arguments that Satan subtly insinuates and incorporates into the temptation. For each argument, I will give you some help to keep your heart.

The pleasure of sin

The first argument is drawn from the pleasure of sin. Satan says,

Oh, here is a pleasure to be enjoyed; the temptation comes with a smiling countenance and a charming voice. What, are you such an apathetic and dull soul as to not feel the powerful charms of pleasure? Who can resist such delights?

Now, your heart may be kept from the danger of this temptation by turning the argument of pleasure back on the tempter, which is done in two ways.

First, agree with Satan that sin is pleasant (you will grant him that), but ask him if the pains of conscience and the flames of hell are pleasant too? Is it pleasant to feel the wounds and throbs of conscience? If so, why did Peter weep so bitterly (Matt 26:75)?[1] Why did David cry of broken bones (Ps 51:8)?[2] Say to Satan:

I hear what you are saying about the pleasure of sin, but I have read what David said about the terrible effects of sin in his Psalm of remembrance:

"For your arrows have sunk into me,
and your hand has come down on me.
There is no soundness in my flesh
because of your indignation;

---

[1] **Matt 26:75** "And Peter remembered the saying of Jesus, 'Before the rooster crows, you will deny me three times.' And he went out and wept bitterly."
[2] **Ps 51:8** "Let me hear joy and gladness; let the bones that you have broken rejoice."

there is no health in my bones
because of my sin.
For my iniquities have gone over my head;
like a heavy burden, they are too heavy for me.
My wounds stink and fester
because of my foolishness,
I am utterly bowed down and prostrate;
all the day I go about mourning.
For my sides are filled with burning,
and there is no soundness in my flesh.
I am feeble and crushed;
I groan because of the tumult of my heart."
(Ps 38:2-8)

Here you can see the true face of sin. If you yield to the temptations of Satan, you must either feel these pangs of conscience or the flames of hell.

Second, why should Satan talk about the pleasure of sin when we know by experience that there is more true pleasure in our sanctification than any act of sin could ever provide. Oh, how sweet it is to please God, to obey conscience, to preserve inward peace, and to be able to say:

In this trial, I have discovered the sincerity of my heart; now I know
I fear the Lord. Now I see that I truly hate sin. Does sin have any
such delights such as these?

This will choke out temptation.

The secrecy of sin

The next argument is drawn from the secrecy of sin. *"Oh,"* says Satan, *"this sin will never publicly disgrace you; no one will know of it."* You can refute this argument and secure your heart as follows. Although Satan claims that no one will know about it, can he find a place devoid of God's presence for you to sin in? In this way, Job secured his heart from this temptation:

> *"Does not he see my ways*
> *and number all my steps?" (Job 31:4)*

Therefore, Job makes a covenant with his eyes (v. 1).[3] Solomon teaches us to reject this temptation with the same argument:

> *"Why should you be intoxicated, my son, with a forbidden woman*
> *and embrace the bosom of an adulteress?*
> *For a man's ways are before the eyes of the Lord,*
> *and he ponders all his paths." (Prov 5:20-21)*

What if you can hide your sin from the eyes of the whole world—you cannot hide it from God. And the time is at hand when the whole world will know it too, for Scripture affirms this:

> *"For nothing is hidden that will not be made manifest, nor is anything secret that will not be known and come to light." (Luke 8:17)*

---

[3] **Job 31:1** "I have made a covenant with my eyes; how then could I gaze at a virgin?"

Besides, your conscience is a thousand witnesses. Do you owe no reverence to yourself? A heathen man once said, "When you are tempted to commit a sin, fear yourself without any other witness." And will you not be afraid to sin before your own conscience? Your conscience always has a reproof in its mouth or a pen in its hand to record your most secret actions.

The profit of sin

The third argument that Satan uses to tempt us is to show us the gain and profit that arises out of sin. He says, *"Why are you so nice and scrupulous? Bend your conscience a little, and you may secure yourself; now is your opportunity."*

To keep your heart from falling into this dangerous snare, respond to the temptation with the following verse:

> *"For what will it profit a man if he gains the whole world and forfeits his soul? Or what shall a man give in return for his soul?"* (Matt 16:26)

Oh, consider your precious soul! Will you hazard it even for all the world? There is an immortal spirit dwelling in your tabernacle of flesh that is more valuable than all earthly things; it will live for all eternity while this world lies in white ashes. You have a soul for which Jesus Christ shed His precious and invaluable blood, and you were sent into the world to care for your soul. Indeed, God has also committed to you the care of your body but (as one has happily expressed it) with this difference: a master commits two things to a servant, the child and the child's clothes, but will the master thank the servant if he pleads, *"I have kept the clothes but I have neglected the life of the child?"*

The smallness of sin

The fourth argument is taken from the smallness of the sin. Satan says, *"It is only a little one, a small matter, a trifle. Who would stand on such subtleties?"* You can refute this argument in three ways.

First, is the majesty of Heaven only a little matter too? If I commit this sin, I must offend and wrong a great God:

"It is he who sits above the circle of the earth,
and its inhabitants are like grasshoppers;
who stretches out the heavens like a curtain,
and spreads them like a tent to dwell in." (Isa 40:22)

Second, is there any such thing as a little Hell to torment little sinners? Are not even the least sinners there filled with the fullness of wrath? Oh, there is great wrath stored up for those whom the world counts as little sinners.

Third, if it is a small sin, then there are only small inducements to commit it. Will you break fellowship with God for a trifle? Will you destroy your peace, wound your conscience, and grieve the Spirit all for nothing? Oh, what madness is this?

The hope for forgiveness

A fifth argument is drawn from the grace of God and the hopes of a pardon. *"Come,"* says Satan, *"God will pass this by as an infirmity; He will not be so extreme as to mark it."*

But keep your heart! Where do you find a promise of mercy to presumptuous sinners? Indeed, for involuntary surprises and unavoidable and lamented infirmities, there is certainly a pardon, but where is the promise to a brazen sinner that sins on the presumption of a pardon? Linger awhile on the following scripture:

"If one person sins unintentionally, he shall offer a female goat a year old for a sin offering. But the person who does anything with a high hand, whether he is native or a sojourner, reviles the Lord, and that person shall be cut off from among his people."
(Numb 15:27, 30)

Furthermore, if God is a God of so much mercy, how can you abuse so good a God? Will you take so glorious an attribute as the mercy of God and abuse it for your sin? Will you wrong Him because He is good? Instead, the goodness of God should lead you to repentance (Rom 2:4).[4]

"But with you there is forgiveness,
that you may be feared." (Ps 130:4)

The example of others

Lastly, sometimes Satan encourages us to sin from the examples of good and holy believers. He says, *"Others have sinned in so many ways and have been restored; therefore, your sin may coexist with grace, and you will be saved, nevertheless."* You can avoid the danger of this temptation and secure your heart by refuting this argument in three ways.

Though good men may commit the same type of sin that you are tempted to, yet did any good man venture to sin upon such a ground and encouragement as this?

Did God record these examples of others for your imitation or warning? Are they not set up as navigation marks that you might avoid the rocks on which others wrecked?

---

[4] **Rom 2:4** "Or do you presume on the riches of his kindness and forbearance and patience, not knowing that God's kindness is meant to lead you to repentance?"

"Now these things took place as examples for us, that we might not desire evil as they did." (1 Cor 10:6)

And are you willing to feel what they felt for their sin? Oh, you dare not follow them in the ways of sin, lest God plunges you into the depths of horror into which He cast them!

In these ways, learn to keep your hearts in the hour of temptation.

Chapter 12

A Season of Doubt

The tenth season that requires special diligence to keep the heart is during a time of spiritual darkness and doubt. When the soul is like Paul on his dangerous voyage with neither sun, moon, nor stars appearing for many days;[1] when God hides His face or when your corruptions dominate and you see little evidence of grace, you might be ready to lose all hope and consolation. At these times, you are ready to draw sad and desperate conclusions about yourself, calling former assurances vain delusions and past experiences hypocrisy. When the serene and clear heavens are overcast with dark clouds, even filled with thunder and horrible tempests, then the poor, pensive soul sits down and weeps forth this sad lamentation:

> *"My endurance has perished; so has my hope from the Lord."*
> *(Lam 3:18)*

Now, during these times, it is a matter of great difficulty to maintain a sincere heart and to keep it from sinking. Therefore, the tenth

---

[1] **Acts 27:20** "When neither sun nor stars appeared for many days, and no small tempest lay on us, all hope of our being saved was at last abandoned."

question is: *in dark and doubting seasons, how can we keep our hearts from entertaining such sad conclusions about our standing, destroying our peace and unfitting us for duty?*

The grounds for our doubts can be reduced to the following two reasons: 1) God's posture toward us, either in a time of an extraordinary affliction or some long and sad desertion, or 2) the soul's posture toward God. And for the latter, we normally argue against the sincerity of our faith in the following ways:

1. From the shame and sorrow of relapsing into the same sins that we had previously risen above.
2. From the feeling that God loves us less.
3. From excessive affections for earthly comforts and enjoyments.
4. From a decrease in the quality of our private duties.
5. From some horrid injection of Satan that greatly confuses us.
6. From God's silence and seeming denial of our requests that we have long prayed for.

These are the common reasons for our despair. Now, to support your heart in this condition, it is necessary to first meditate on some general truths that can settle your trembling and doubting soul. Then you must be correctly instructed about prolonged afflictions and feelings of desertion.

Comforting truths

The following general truths must be understood by all poor and doubting souls:

First, an act of hypocrisy does not make you a hypocrite. Every work and appearance of hypocrisy does not currently prove that the person in whom it is found is a hypocrite. You must carefully distinguish between the *presence* and *predominance* of hypocrisy; for there are remnants of deceitfulness in the best hearts. David and Peter had sad experiences with this truth, yet the perpetual frame and general bent of their hearts were upright—they were not counted as hypocrites.

Second, you may be an enemy of your own peace. We must equally hear what can be said *for us* as *against us*. It is the sin of upright hearts to sometimes use an overly rigid and merciless severity against themselves. They do not objectively consider the case for their own souls. It is like Solomon's words about riches:

> "One pretends to be rich, yet has nothing;
> another pretends to be poor, yet has great wealth." *(Prov 13:7)*

The damning sin of self-flattering hypocrites is to see their condition as better than it is, but it is the sin and folly of some upright Christians to see their condition as worse than it is. Why should you be an enemy to your own peace? Why do you read the evidence of God's love for your soul as a man does a book that he intends to refute? Why do you study to find evasions to reject those comforts that are due to you? It is said of Joseph that he was told to put away his betrothed Mary, not knowing that the holy one conceived in her was done so by the Holy Spirit. And this may be your case.

Third, you may charge yourself falsely. Many saints have charged and condemned themselves for that which God will never charge them with nor condemn them for. Isaiah asks does the Lord "harden our heart, so that we fear you not?" (Isa 63:17);[2] and yet the previous verse demonstrates that their hearts were not so hardened (v. 16).[3] Godly Bradford wrote himself off as a hypocrite, yet God certainly acquitted him of that charge.

Fourth, each misstep is not grounds for doubt. Every action that is a cause for grief for the people of God is not a sufficient ground for questioning their sincerity. There are many more things to *trouble* you than there are to *stumble* you. If you question all that God ever did through you on every sinful slip and failure, your life will be made up of continual doubts and fears, and you will never attain a settled peace nor live the life of praise and thankfulness that the Gospel calls for.

Fifth, your soul is not always a suitable judge. During the dark day of desertion, when the soul is despondent, and in the stormy day of temptation, when the soul is flustered, it is utterly unfit to judge its own condition. "Ponder in your own hearts on your beds, and be silent" (Ps 4:4). Instead, this is a season for watching and resisting rather than judging and determining.

Sixth, sins do not result in the loss of your salvation. Every breach of peace with God is not a breach of the covenant of God. A wife has many weaknesses and failings that often grieve and displease her husband, but for the most part, she is faithful and truly loves him. These

---

[2] **Isa 63:17** "O Lord, why do you make us wander from your ways and harden our heart, so that we fear you not? Return for the sake of your servants, the tribes of your heritage."

[3] **Isa 63:16** "For you are our Father, though Abraham does not know us, and Israel does not acknowledge us; you, O Lord, are our Father, our Redeemer from of old is your name."

failings may cause him to alter his demeanor, but it would never cause him to withdraw his love or abandon the relationship.

> "Return, faithless Israel,
> declares the Lord.
> I will not look on you in anger,
> for I am merciful,
> declares the Lord;
> I will not be angry forever."
> (Jer 3:12)

Lastly, run toward God. Whatever your sin or trouble, it should drive you *to God* rather than *from God.* "Pardon my guilt, for it is great" (Ps 25:11). Suppose it is true that you have sinned and broken fellowship with God; yet it is a false conclusion to say that you should be discouraged, as if there were no help from God.

When you have carefully meditated on these seven establishing truths, if your doubts still remain, then consider how you may address the particular grounds of those doubts.

Great affliction

One primary source of our doubts happens when extraordinary suffering comes on us. In these moments, you are ready to conclude that the Lord has no regard or love for your soul. But I would not want you to conclude this until you are able to satisfactorily answer the following three questions.

If great trouble and afflictions are marks of God's hatred, would that not mean that license and constant prosperity are tokens of his love? For with opposite things, there is an opposite reason and cause. But is this true in reality? Does not Scripture say quite otherwise? "The prosperity of fools shall destroy them" (Prov 1:32, KJV), and the Psalmist laments:

> "I was envious of the arrogant
> when I saw the prosperity of the wicked." (Ps 73:3)

Also, do you dare draw the same conclusions on others who have been much more afflicted than yourself? If this argument holds for you, then it also applies to everyone in your condition. In fact, the greater the affliction of any child of God, the more strongly the argument would hold. But then woe to David, Job, Heman,[4] and Paul who all experienced great suffering.

And had God exempted only you from the suffering that all His people feel, would that not be stronger grounds for you to doubt than this? This is especially true considering the teaching of Scripture:

> "If you are left without discipline, in which all have participated, then you are illegitimate children and not sons." (Heb 12:8)

Oh, how our Father is put to the test by willful children! If He afflicts, some cry that they are not loved when they are exempt from the afflictions, whereas others question His love for being afflicted. Surely, you have other work to do under the rod than this.

Fear of desertion

The other cause of these doubts happens when it seems the Lord is hiding His face from you. In these times, you rashly infer that He has

---

[4] See Psalm 88.

no love for you because your condition is miserable, dark, and uncomfortable. Before you draw such rash conclusions, see what answers you can give to the following four questions.

First, if any action of God toward His people can be seen in both a positive and harsh light, why should we not interpret it in the best sense? And is this not true? May He not have a design of love as well of discipline in this experience? May He not depart for a season and not forever? You are not the first person who has mistaken God's purpose in desertion.[5]

> *"But Zion said, 'The Lord has forsaken me;*
> *my Lord has forgotten me.'" (Isa 49:14)*

But was this true? Far from it!

> *"Can a woman forget her nursing child,*
> *that she should have no compassion on the son of her womb?*
> *Even these may forget,*
> *yet I will not forget you." (v. 15)*

Second, do you find the marks of an absolute and final desertion upon your spirit that makes you conclude you are abandoned? Do you find that your heart is inclined to forsake God? Are you less conscientious and sensitive about your sin? If so, these are sad signs indeed. But, if in this dark hour, you are as aware of sin as ever and as much resolved to cleave to God as ever, saying,

---

[5] *Desertion* here refers to our feelings of the loss of God's presence or activity in our lives rather than actual abandonment.

I cannot, I will not forsake God. Let Him do what He will with me. Oh, no, I cannot.

If your heart works like this, it must be only a partial, limited, and temporary desertion. By these thoughts, God still keeps His interest in your heart, which is a sure sign He will return and visit you again.

Third, are your feelings a competent judge of God's actions and designs? Can we safely rely on our feelings after so many discoveries of how fallible they are? Is this a sound argument:

If God had any love for my soul, and if His love remained, I would feel it now as I did in former times. But I cannot feel it; therefore, it is absolutely gone.

Do you not know that the sun keeps its course in the heavens even when the weather is dull and overcast and you cannot see it? And may it not be the same with the love of God?

*"Let him who walks in darkness
and has no light
trust in the name of the Lord
and rely on his God." (Isa 50:10)*

Is this not the same as concluding in winter, when the flowers have hidden their beautiful heads underground, that they are quite dead and gone, because you cannot find them in December where you saw them in May?

Lastly, does the Lord not care about breaking His children's hearts and His own promises too? Does He have no regard to either? If He never returns, then you make God out to be a liar:

"For I will not contend forever,
nor will I always be angry;
for the spirit would grow faint before me,
and the breath of life that I made.
Because of the iniquity of his unjust gain I was angry,
I struck him; I hid my face and was angry,
but he went on backsliding in the way of his own heart."
(Isa 57:16-17)

"I will never leave you nor forsake you." (Heb 13:5)

Therefore, we cannot draw such discouraging, heart-sinking conclusions from God's dealings with us, either in our afflictions or His silence. Next, let us see whether our own actions can provide the grounds for our doubts.

Repeated sins

When you fall again into the same sins from which you had formerly risen from with repentance and resolution, you are tempted to view the sin as habitual—something that should not be the case for God's children. Therefore, the upright soul trembles at this and is ready to call all its former repentance and opposition as just the actions of a hypocrite. But be comforted, poor trembling heart.

If this is so, how does it come to pass that Christ used such a patient tone with the Disciples when he found them sleeping for the third time after he had corrected them each other time?[6] And how is it that we find so many promises in Scripture that are not only for the first sins but also to the backsliding sins of God's people?

---

[6] See Matthew 26:36-46.

"'Return, O faithless sons;
I will heal your faithlessness.'
'Behold, we come to you,
for you are the Lord our God.'" (Jer 3:22)

"I will heal their apostasy;
I will love them freely,
for my anger has turned from them." (Hos 14:4)

And do you not find that your repentance and concern are renewed as often as your guilt is renewed? Are you not more troubled the more often you sin? It is not so in a life that is accustomed to sinning, which is described well by Bernard. He says that when a man first sins grievously, it seems unbearable; he seems to descend alive into hell. In the process of time, it seems not unbearable but heavy, and the difference between the two is not small. Next, it becomes light; his conscience smites only faintly, and he does not feel the stripes of it. Then he is not only completely insensible of it, but that which was once bitter and displeasing has now become sweet and pleasing to some degree. Then it is turned into custom, and it not only pleases but daily pleases. Lastly, custom is turned into nature, and he cannot be pulled away from it but defends and pleads for it. This is the way of habitual sinning, and it is the way of the wicked. But this is quite contrary to our condition.

Finally, are you sure from Scripture that a good man may not relapse again and again into the same sin? It is true for extraordinary sins, which are typically not repeated. David did not commit adultery again, Paul never again persecuted the Church, and Peter never denied Christ again. But I speak of ordinary sins. Job's friend were good men, yet he said, "These ten times you have cast reproach upon me" (Job 19:3). So then, there can be no such conclusions from this first ground of doubting.

Fear of losing God's love

Another cause of doubts is when you find yourself declining and withering in your desire for spiritual things. You say,

Oh, if I had been planted as a healthy seed, I would now be like a green olive tree in the house of my God; but my branches wither, therefore my root is bad.

But consider the following questions. Is it possible that you could be mistaken about the decay of grace and the fading of your affections? What if they are not as quick and ravishing as they were at first? May this not be made up by the spirituality and stability of them now?

"It is my prayer that your love may abound more and more, with knowledge and all discernment." (Phil 1:9)

Your faith may be more solid but not so passionate. Or, perhaps you err by looking forward to what you will become rather than backward to what you once were. Ames explained this well: we discern the growth of grace as the growth of plants—rather than seeing them grow, we perceive that they *have grown.*

But even if it is indeed as you claim, must it necessarily follow that the root of the grace is not in you? David's last ways are distinguished from his first (Chron 17:3),[7] and yet in both first and last, he was a holy man. The church of Ephesus was charged by Christ for leaving her first love, and yet there is a golden candlestick and many precious saints from that church (Rev 2:1-7).

---

[7] **2 Chron 17:3** "The Lord was with Jehoshaphat, because he walked in the earlier ways of his father David. He did not seek the Baals."

Excessive desires

Another ground for these sad conclusions is the excess of affections for some earthly enjoyments. You fear that you love the world more than God, turning your love for Him into hypocrisy. This is especially true if you sometimes feel stronger and more tangible longings of your heart to some earthly comforts than you do to heavenly ones. Consequently, you fear your soul is not upright. But consider the following.

Is it not possible that you may love God more solidly and strongly than this world, and yet your affections for created things are sometimes moved more forcibly than they are toward God? A rooted malice argues for a stronger hatred than a sudden more violent passion; in the same way, we must not measure our love for God by the violent motion of it now and then, but by the depth of the root and the constancy of its actions. David was so passionately moved after the death of Absalom that Joab concludes that "if Absalom were alive and all of us were dead today, then you would be pleased" (2 Sam 19:6). But this was argued more like a soldier than a philosopher.

If you really love created things for themselves and make them your aim (and religion only a means), then the conclusion is rightly applied to you. But if you love these things in reference to God and see everything in relation to Him, this is consistent with sincere love for God (though sometimes your affections can offend in their excess). To love the things of this world inordinately, putting them in God's place and making them your primary end, this is the love of a carnal heart. But to love them immoderately—that is, to give them more affection than we ought—is sometimes the sin of the best hearts.

And have there not been many saints who fear as you do that if it came to a trial between Christ and the creature, that they should forsake Christ in favor of the creature? And yet, when they have been brought to that dilemma, they were able to cast aside all the world for Christ.

Many of the martyrs had such fears, and they also overcame. The power of love is best seen at a moment of parting; there may be more love for Christ in your soul than you are currently aware of; and if God brings you to such a trial, you may see it.

Struggles in private duties

The fourth source of these sad conclusions is when you find your heart is at times more constrained in private rather than public duties. You think if your soul were sincere, it would have a uniform approach to duty; and on this basis, you fear that you are a pharisee. It is indeed sad that we should ever find our hearts restrained in private. However, consider the following points.

Do not all of your increases in duty, whether public or private, depend upon the Spirit, who is the Lord of influences? And depending on what He gives out or holds back, so are you enlarged or constrained. So what if He is sometimes pleased to give to you in public what He withholds in private duties? If the inadequacy of your heart is indeed a burden and if your soul is never satisfied in any duty without communion with God, does this argue that you are a hypocrite?

Also, do you not conscientiously make time for private duties and set yourself before the Lord in them? Indeed, if you live in a constant neglect of private duties or carelessly perform them, that would be a discouraging sign; but when you have conscientiously performed them and often met with God in them, it does not mean you are insincere when that communion is sometimes interrupted.

Besides, may there not at times be some things in public duties, which are lacking in private, that raise and help your affections. God may sometimes make use of the melting affections of those whom you listen to or pray for as a simple instrument to move your affections. This opportunity is missing in private duties. Therefore, no such inference can be drawn.

Satan's lies

Another ground for our doubts is from those horrid injections of Satan that greatly perplex the soul. By his insinuations, you say, *"What a heart I have! Can grace be where such sins are present?"*

Yes, grace may be where such thoughts are found but not where they are lodged and consented to. Do you cry out under the burden and enter your protest in Heaven against them? Do you strive to keep up holy and reverent thoughts of God? Then this is a violation rather than a voluntary prostitution of the heart.

Unanswered prayers

The last ground for these sad conclusions is the Lord's long silence and seeming denial of that for which we have long prayed. You think that if God had any regard for your soul, He would have heard your cries before now. In the absence of an answer from Him, you are tempted to believe you have no part of Him. But be still, doubting soul!

Have not many saints stumbled on this stone before you?

"I had said in my alarm,
'I am cut off from your sight.'
But you heard the voice of my pleas for mercy
when I cried to you for help." (Ps 31:22)

"You have wrapped yourself with a cloud
so that no prayer can pass through." (Lam 3:44)

"Then I said, 'I am driven away
from your sight;
yet I shall again look

upon your holy temple.'" (Jonah 2:4)

May you not be mistaken in your conclusions as they were?

Although God's abhorrence and final rejection of an individual's prayer is an argument of His rejection of the person that prays, should we dare conclude this from a mere suspension of the answer?

"And will not God give justice to his elect, who cry to him day and night? Will he delay long over them?" (Luke 18:7)

And do you not see that there are some signs appearing in your soul even while God suspends His answer that argues that your prayers are not rejected by Him? For example, though no answer comes, you find that you are still resolved to wait; you would not dare to say as the profane wretch did: "This trouble is from the Lord! Why should I wait for the Lord any longer?" (2 Kings 6:33). Or you can still vindicate the justice of God and lay the reason and cause of His silence upon yourself as David did:

"O my God, I cry by day, but you do not answer,
and by night, but I find no rest.
Yet you are holy,
enthroned on the praises of Israel." (Ps 22:2-3)

Or you may find that the suspension of God's answer makes you look into your own heart to see what evils might be obstructing your prayers. This was the case with God's people in Lamentations:

"Though I call and cry for help,
he shuts out my prayer." (Lam 3:8)

And what is their response?

> *"Let us test and examine our ways,*
> *and return to the Lord!" (v. 40)*

Therefore, you cannot use this reason to conclude that God has no love for your soul.

Thus, I have shown you how to keep your heart in a dark and doubting season from those desperate conclusions of unbelief. God forbid that any false believers should encourage themselves with these arguments! It is sad that when we give saints and sinners their proper portions, each of them is so prone to take up the other's part.

Chapter 13

A Season of Persecution

The eleventh special season that calls for diligence to keep our hearts is when religious persecution comes to a height. Then, look to your hearts:

"All these are but the beginning of the birth pains. Then they will deliver you up to tribulation and put you to death, and you will be hated by all nations for my name's sake. And then many will fall away and betray one another and hate one another."
(Mat 24:8-10)

When religious persecution grows hot, blessed is the one who is not offended by Christ. Troubles are at a height:

- When your nearest friends and relations forsake and leave you, and you are left alone (Mic 7:5-6;[1] 2 Tim 4:16[2]).
- When you resist sin to the point of shedding blood (Heb 12:4).[3]
- When you are tempted in your sufferings (Heb 11:37).[4]
- When eminent professing Christians turn aside and desert the cause of Christ (2 John 2:19).[5]
- When God hides His face in an hour of suffering (Jer 17:17).[6]
- When Satan falls upon you with strong temptations to question the reasons for your sufferings or your soul's share in Christ.

Now, at these times, it is hard to keep your heart from turning back and your feet from avoiding God's paths. Therefore, the next question is: *how can we be kept from falling away under the greatest sufferings for the Gospel?* If the bitterness of sufferings ever cause your soul to dislike the way of God and take up thoughts of forsaking it, compose your

---

[1] **Mic 7:5-6** "Put no trust in a neighbor; have no confidence in a friend; guard the doors of your mouth from her who lies in your arms; for the son treats the father with contempt, the daughter rises up against her mother, the daughter-in-law against her mother-in-law; a man's enemies are the men of his own house."

[2] **2 Tim 4:16** "At my first defense no one came to stand by me, but all deserted me. May it not be charged against them!"

[3] **Heb 12:4** "In your struggle against sin you have not yet resisted to the point of shedding your blood."

[4] **Heb 11:37** "They were stoned, they were sawn in two, they were killed with the sword. They went about in skins of sheep and goats, destitute, afflicted, mistreated."

[5] **2 John 2:19** "They went out from us, but they were not of us; for if they had been of us, they would have continued with us. But they went out, that it might become plain that they all are not of us."

[6] **Jer 17:17** "Be not a terror to me; you are my refuge in the day of disaster."

heart under that temptation by solemnly asking these eight questions of it.

First, are you willing to reproach and dishonor Christ and the Gospel by deserting Him at such a time as this? This will proclaim to all the world that, regardless of how much you have boasted of the promises, when it comes to a trial, you dare not risk anything on them. Consider how this will open the mouths of Christ's enemies to blaspheme? Oh, it would be better not to be born than that worthy name should be blasphemed through you! Will you supply the victories of the enemy? Will you bring joy to Hell? If you just value the name of Christ as much as many wicked men value their own names, you will not endure seeing it exposed to such contempt. Will proud dust and ashes venture death—and even Hell—rather than suffer a blot upon their name? And will you venture nothing to save the honor and reputation of Christ?

Second, do you dare violate the conscience to save the flesh? Who will comfort you when your conscience pangs you? What comfort is there in life, liberty, or friends, when peace is taken away from the inner man? When Constantius threatened to cut off the hand of Samosatenus because he would not comply on a point that was against his conscience, Samosatenus held up both hands to the messenger, saying, "He can cut off both rather than I will do it." Farewell, all peace, joy, and comfort from that day forward! Did Zimri have peace after murdering his master?[7] Did Judas have peace? Did Spira have peace? And will you have peace if you tread in their steps? Oh, consider what you do!

---

[7] A reference to Jezebel's words in 2 Kings 9:31. For the backstory of the reign and fall of Zimri, who was a king of Israel, see 1 Kings 16:1-20.

Third, isn't the public mission of Christ and the Gospel infinitely more important than any private interests of your own? One famous account of Terentius (Captain to Adrian the Emperor) is that he presented a petition to Adrian that the Christians might have a temple for themselves to worship God apart from the Arians. The Emperor tore his petition and threw it away, telling him to ask something for himself, and it would be granted. But Terentius modestly gathered up the pieces of his petition again and told him that if he could not be heard in God's cause, he would never ask anything for himself. Yes, even Tully, though a heathen, said that he would not accept even immortality itself against the commonwealth. Oh, if we had a greater sense of the public cause of Christ, we would not have such cowardly spirits.

Fourth, did Jesus Christ treat you this way when, for your sake, He exposed Himself to far greater sufferings than you face now? His sufferings were great indeed. He suffered in all His offices from all hands—not only in His body but also in His soul. In fact, the sufferings of His soul were the very soul of His sufferings. See the bloody sweat in the garden,[8] and witness the heart-melting and heaven-rending outcry from the cross:

"My God, my God, why have you forsaken me?" (Matt 27:46)

And yet, He did not flinch but "endured the cross, despising the shame" (Heb 12:2).[9] Alas! What are our sufferings compared with Christ's? He has drunk up all the vinegar and gall that would make our sufferings bitter. When one of the martyrs was asked why he was so merry at his

---

[8] See Luke 22:44.

[9] **Heb 12:2** "Looking to Jesus, the founder and perfecter of our faith, who for the joy that was set before him endured the cross, despising the shame, and is seated at the right hand of the throne of God."

death, he said, *"Oh, it is because the soul of Christ was so heavy at His death. Did Christ bear such a burden for me with unbroken patience and constancy? And will I shrink back for momentary and light afflictions for Him?"*

Fifth, isn't eternal life worth the suffering of a moment's pain? If we suffer with Him, we will reign with Him. Oh, see how men risk life and limb for a fading crown or wade through seas of blood for a throne. Yet will we venture nothing and suffer nothing for the crown of glory that never fades away? My dog will follow my horse's heels from morning to night and take many a weary step through mud and dirt rather than leave me, even though at night all he gets by it is bones and blows. If my soul had any true greatness or any sparks of generosity in it, it would scorn the sufferings along the way for the glory of the end, breaking down all obstacles in its way. Look and see, by the eye of faith, the forerunner who has already entered and is standing, as it were, upon the walls of heaven with the crown in His hand, saying, *he who overcomes will inherit all things* (James 1:12).[10] Come on, then, my soul, come on:

"To those who by patience in well-doing seek for glory and honor and immortality, he will give eternal life." (Rom 2:7)

Sixth, can you so easily cast off the society of the saints and give the right hand of fellowship to the wicked? How can you part with such lovely companions as they have been? How often have you benefited

---

[10] **James 1:12** "Blessed is the man who remains steadfast under trial, for when he has stood the test he will receive the crown of life, which God has promised to those who love him."

from the counsel of the wicked or been refreshed, warmed, and energized by their company (Eccl 4:10-11)?[11] How often have you fasted and prayed for them, and what sweet counsel have you taken from them? Have they kept you company as you have gone to the house of God? And will you now shake hands with them and say, *"farewell, all you saints forever, I will never be among you again; come drunkards, swearers, blasphemers, and persecutors: you will be my everlasting companions?"* Oh, rather let your body and soul be torn in two than you should ever say this to "the excellent ones of the earth, in whom is all my delight" (Ps 16:3).[12]

Seventh, have you seriously considered the terrible condemnation against backsliders in Scripture? Oh, do you dare let your heart turn away in light of such pointed threats such as these?

> *"Thus says the Lord:*
> *'Cursed is the man who trusts in man*
> *and makes flesh his strength,*
> *whose heart turns away from the Lord.*
> *He is like a shrub in the desert,*
> *and shall not see any good come.*
> *He shall dwell in the parched places of the wilderness,*
> *in an uninhabited salt land.'" (Jer 17:5-6)*

---

[11] **Eccl 4:10-11** "For if they fall, one will lift up his fellow. But woe to him who is alone when he falls and has not another to lift him up! Again, if two lie together, they keep warm, but how can one keep warm alone?"

[12] **Ps 16:3** "As for the saints in the land, they are the excellent ones, in whom is all my delight."

"For if we go on sinning deliberately after receiving the knowledge of the truth, there no longer remains a sacrifice for sins, but a fearful expectation of judgment, and a fury of fire that will consume the adversaries." (Heb 14:26-27)

"But my righteous one shall live by faith,
and if he shrinks back,
my soul has no pleasure in him." (Heb 14:38)

Oh, who dares draw back when God has hedged up the way with such terrible threats as these!

Lastly, will you be able to look Christ in the face on the day of judgment if you desert Him now?

"For whoever is ashamed of me and of my words in this adulterous and sinful generation, of him will the Son of Man also be ashamed when he comes in the glory of his Father with the holy angels." (Mark 8:38)

In a little while, you will see the sign of the Son of Man coming on the clouds of Heaven with power and great glory; the trumpet will sound, and the dead, both small and great—even all who sleep in the dust—will awake and come before that great white throne on which Christ will sit in that day. And now, simply imagine that you saw the trembling knees and quivering lips of guilty sinners. Imagine that you heard the dreadful sentence of the Judge upon them, "Depart from me, you cursed" (Matt 25:41),[13] followed by crying, weeping, wailing, and the wringing of hands.

Would you desert Christ now to prolong a poor, miserable life on earth? If the Word of God is true and if the sayings of Christ are sealed and faithful, this will be the portion of unbelievers. It is an easy thing to stop the mouth of conscience now, but will it be easy to stop the mouth of the Judge of them? Therefore, keep your heart lest it departs from the living God.

---

[13] **Matt 25:41** "Then he will say to those on his left, 'Depart from me, you cursed, into the eternal fire prepared for the devil and his angels.'"

Chapter 14

A Season of Sickness

T he twelfth season that requires us to diligently search our hearts and keep them with the greatest care is a time of sickness. When a child of God draws close to eternity—when there are only a few grains of sand left to fall from the upper part of the hourglass—then Satan busily engages himself. You may say of Satan what is said of the natural serpent: he is never seen at his full length until dying. And since he cannot win the soul from God, his great design now is to discourage the soul and make it unwilling to go to God. But the gracious soul with Jacob should then rouse itself upon its deathbed and rejoice that the marriage day of the Lamb is almost here. You should say with dying Austen, "I despise life to be with Christ." Or consider Milius who, when asked if he were willing to die, replied, "Oh! The one who is unwilling to die is the one who is unwilling to go to Christ."

And yet, how often—indeed, too often—do we see the people of God shrinking from death and reluctant to depart? How loth are some to take death by the cold hand? If we were indulged with the freedom to not be dissolved until we dissolved ourselves, when would we say with Paul, "My desire is to depart and be with Christ" (Phil 1:23)?

Therefore, the last question is: *in times of sickness, how can we get our hearts freed from all earthly engagements and persuade them into a willingness to die?* And at such a time as this, there are seven arguments that I will urge upon the people of God to make them cheerfully entertain the messengers of death—to die as well as live like Saints.

The harmlessness of death

First, consider that death is harmless to the people of God. Though it keeps its dart, it has lost its sting. A saint may "play over the hole of the cobra and…put his hand on the adder's den" (Isa 11:8). Death is the adder or cobra, and grace is his hole or den; saints do not need to fear to put their hand boldly into it. It has left and lost its sting in the side of Christ: "O death, where is your victory? O death, where is your sting?" (1 Cor 15:55).

Why are you afraid, oh saint, that this sickness will be your death, as long as you know that the death of Christ is the death of death? Indeed, if you did die in your sins (John 8:21);[1] if death as a king did reign over you (Rom 5:14);[2] if it could feed on you as the lion does on his prey (Ps 49:14);[3] and if hell followed the pale horse (Rev 6:8),[4] then you might reasonably startle and shrink back from it. But when God has

---

[1] **John 8:21** "So he said to them again, "I am going away, and you will seek me, and you will die in your sin. Where I am going, you cannot come.""

[2] **Rom 5:14** "Yet death reigned from Adam to Moses, even over those whose sinning was not like the transgression of Adam, who was a type of the one who was to come."

[3] **Ps 49:14** "Like sheep they are appointed for Sheol; death shall be their shepherd, and the upright shall rule over them in the morning. Their form shall be consumed in Sheol, with no place to dwell."

[4] **Rev 6:8** "And I looked, and behold, a pale horse! And its rider's name was Death, and Hades followed him. And they were given authority over a fourth of the earth, to kill with sword and with famine and with pestilence and by wild beasts of the earth."

removed your sins from you "as far as the east is from the west" (Ps 103:12);[5] when there is no longer any evil to face in death but bodily pain; and when the Scriptures represent it to you with such harmless and easy comparisons, such as removing your clothes and lying down to sleep,[6] why should you be afraid? There is as much of a difference between death for the people of God and others as there is between a unicorn's horn when it is upon the head of that fierce beast and when it is in the apothecary's shop, where it is made beneficial and medicinal.

The necessity of death

To keep your heart from shrinking back at such a time as this, consider the necessity of death for the full fruition of God's plan. Whether you are willing to die or not, I assure you that there is no other way to obtain the full satisfaction of your soul or to complete its happiness. Until the hand of death does you the kind favor of drawing aside the curtain of the flesh, your soul cannot see God; this physical life stands between you and Him.

> "We know that while we are at home in the body we are away from the Lord." (2 Cor 5:6)

Your body must be refined and cast into a new mold; otherwise, the new wine of heavenly glory would break it. When Paul had entered his highest rapture and "heard things that cannot be told" (2 Cor 12:4), he was only a bystander, a looker-on, who was not admitted into the company as one of them; but as the angels are in our assemblies, so was Paul in that glorious assembly above. And yet even as an observer, he was

---

[5] **Ps 103:12** "As far as the east is from the west, so far does he remove our transgressions from us."

[6] See 2 Corinthians 5:1-4 and Isaiah 57:1-2.

required to be, in a sense, taken out of the body and unclothed for a short time to have a glimpse of that glory before returning to put on his bodily clothes again!

Oh then, who would not be willing to die for the full sight and enjoyment of God? I think your soul should look and sigh like a prisoner through the bars of this mortality.

> "Oh, that I had wings like a dove! I would fly away and be at rest."
> (Ps 55:6)

Most unbelievers need patience to die, but as saints who understand what death admits us to, we should instead need patience to live! When we are on our deathbed, I think we should often look and listen for the Lord's coming. And when we receive the news of His approaching charge, we should say:

> "The voice of my beloved!
> Behold, he comes,
> leaping over the mountains,
> bounding over the hills." (Song 2:8)

The superiority of the next life

Another argument to persuade you to this willingness to die is the reality of an immediate succession of a more excellent and glorious life. It is only a wink, and you will see God. Your happiness will not be deferred until the resurrection; as soon as the body is dead, the gracious soul is swallowed up in life.

"But if Christ is in you, although the body is dead because of sin, the Spirit is life because of righteousness. If the Spirit of him who raised Jesus from the dead dwells in you, he who raised Christ Jesus from the dead will also give life to your mortal bodies through his Spirit who dwells in you." (Rom 8:10-11)

In a few moments after you have set off from this shore, your soul will be wafted over upon the wings of Angels to the other shore of a glorious eternity. Paul said,

"My desire is to depart and be with Christ, for that is far better."
(Phil 1:23)

Do the soul and body die together, as Beryllus taught? Or do they sleep until the Resurrection as others have groundlessly imagined? If so, it would be madness for Paul to desire to depart for the enjoyment of Christ. For if this were so, he would have enjoyed more of Christ while his soul dwelt in its fleshly Tabernacle than he would out of it.

According to Scripture, the soul only has two modes of living—the life of *faith*, and the life of *vision* (2 Cor 5:7).[7] Those two divide all time, both present and future, between them (1 Cor 13:12).[8] When faith ends at death, if sight does not immediately follow, what will become of the unbodied soul? But blessed be God for this great heart-establishing truth that is clearly revealed in Scripture in the promises of Christ:

"And he said to him, 'Truly, I say to you, today you will be with me in paradise.'" (Luke 23:43)

---

[7] **2 Cor 5:7** "For we walk by faith, not by sight."
[8] **1 Cor 13:12** "For now we see in a mirror dimly, but then face to face. Now I know in part; then I shall know fully, even as I have been fully known."

"And if I go and prepare a place for you, I will come again and will take you to myself, that where I am you may be also." (John 14:3)

Oh, what a change a few moments will make upon your condition! Rouse up, dying saint. When your soul has come out a little farther, you will stand like Abraham at the door of your tent, and the angels of God will soon be with you. The souls of the elect are, in a sense, put out for the angels to nurse, and when they die, the angels carry them home again to their Father's house. If an angel was caused to fly swiftly to bring a saint the answer of his prayer (Dan 9:21), how much more will the angels come quickly from heaven to receive and transfer the praying soul itself?

The rescue of death

One consideration that may contribute to your willingness to die is to consider that by death God often hides His people out of the way of all the temptations and troubles that are coming on the earth.

"Blessed are the dead who die in the Lord from now on." (Rev 14:13)

When some extraordinary calamities are coming upon the world, it is God's typical way to set His people out of harm's way beforehand.

"For the righteous man is taken away from calamity." (Isa 57:1)

Micah describes such an evil time: "they all lie in wait for blood, and each hunts the other with a net" (Mic 7:2); but before that, God by an act of favor takes His people home. Do you know what evil may be coming on the earth that you are so reluctant to leave? Your God removes you for your great advantage; you are disbanded by death and called off the field. Other poor saints must stand against it and endure a great fight of afflictions.

It has been noted that Methuselah died the year before the flood, Augustine died shortly before the sacking of Hippo, and Pareus died just before Heidelberg was taken. Luther observed that all of the Apostles died before the destruction of Jerusalem, and Luther himself died before the wars broke out in Germany. It may be that the Lord sees your tender heart cannot endure to see the misery or bear the temptations that are coming, and he is, therefore, gathering you to your grave in peace. And yet, will you cry, "Oh, spare me a little longer?"

The advantage of death

If your heart still hangs back, consider the great advantages that you will have by death—more than any that you have ever enjoyed on earth. Consider both your communion with God and your communion with saints.

For your communion with God, the time of perfecting has now come. Your soul will shortly stand before the face of God, whose glory will immediately shine and beam forth upon it. Here on Earth, your soul is more remote from God, and the beams of His glory strike it only obliquely and feebly. But soon it will be in a direct line, and there the sun will stand still as it did in Gibeon.[9] There will be no cloud nor any diminishing of it. Oh, how it will fill your soul with desires of being unclothed!

As for the enjoyment of the saints, we certainly have fellowship with them here of a lower form; but that fellowship is so affected by remaining corruptions that there is no satisfaction in it. Just as it is the greatest plague that could fall on a hypocrite to live in a pure church, so also it is the greatest vexation for the spirit of a saint to live in a corrupt

---

[9] See Joshua 10:1-14.

and disordered church. But when death has admitted you into that glorious assembly of the spirits of the righteous made perfect, you will have the desire of your heart. Here, you cannot fully connect with one another (in fact, you cannot fully connect with your own soul). Oh, what discord, arguing, and censuring are here? But what perfect, blessed harmony is there? In Heaven, each saint loves another as himself; they are altogether lovely. Oh, my soul, hurry away from the lions' den and the mountains of Bether; run to those mountains of myrrh and the hill of frankincense. You are now going to your own people, as the apostle's phrase describes:

> *"Yes, we are of good courage, and we would rather be away from the body and at home with the Lord." (2 Cor 5:8)*

The comfort of death

If all this will not convince you, consider the heavy burdens that death will ease from your shoulders. In this tabernacle, we groan and are burdened.

As for physical ailments, how true do we find the saying of Theophrastus: the soul pays a dear rent for the tenement it now lives in. But our glorified bodies will not be plagued by any infirmities. Death is the best physician; it will cure you of all diseases at once.

Indwelling sin makes us groan from the depths of our being:

> *"Wretched man that I am! Who will deliver me from this body of death?" (Rom 7:24)*

But "one who has died has been set free from sin" (Rom 6:7). Justification has destroyed the damning power of sin, and sanctification has defeated its reigning power; but glorification destroys its very being and existence.

Here we also groan under temptations, but as soon as we are out of the body, we are out of reach of temptation. The moment you get into Heaven, you may say, *"Now, Satan, I am here where you cannot come!"* For, as the damned in Hell are so fixed in sin and misery that their condition cannot be altered, so also glorified saints are so fixed in holiness and glory that they cannot be shaken.

Here we groan under various troubles and afflictions, but there the days of our mourning are ended. God will wipe away all tears and dry our eyes. Oh, then! Let us hurry away that we may be at rest.

Our groundless arguments to stay

If you still linger like Lot in Sodom, then lastly examine all the pleas and pretenses that you make for a longer time on earth. Why are you unwilling to die?

You might object that you are concerned about what will become of your family and relations when you are gone. If you are troubled about their bodies and outward condition, why are you not satisfied with the following scripture:

> *"Leave your fatherless children; I will keep them alive; and let your widows trust in me." (Jer 49:11)*

In his last will and testament, Luther said the following prayer: *"Lord, you have given me wife and children; I have nothing to leave them, but I commit them to You, Oh Father of the fatherless and judge of widows. Nourish, keep, and teach them."* Or are you troubled for their souls? You cannot convert them if you should live, and God can make your prayers and counsels to live and take effect on them when you are dead.

You might also object that you want to live to serve God more in the world. But if he has no more service for you to do here, why should you not say with David,

"If he says, 'I have no pleasure in you,' behold, here I am, let him do to me what seems good to him." (2 Sam 15:26)

In this world, you may have no more to do, but He is calling you to a higher service and employment in Heaven. What you want to do for Him here, He can do better by other hands.

Or you might object that you are not yet fully ready, as a bride completely adorned for the bridegroom. However, your justification is complete already, though your sanctification is not so; and the way to make it so is to die. For until then, it will have its defects and deficiencies.

Lastly, you might object because of assurance. If you had greater assurance, you could be willing to die now. Yes, here it weighs heavy; but consider that a hearty willingness to leave all the world to be freed from sin and be with God is the next step to that desired assurance. No carnal person was ever willing to die upon this ground.

And so, I have finished those cases which so deeply concern the people of God throughout various conditions of life, teaching you how to keep your hearts through them all. I will next apply the whole teaching.

Chapter 15

Application and Exhortation

You have heard that the great work of a Christian is to keep the heart, in which the very soul and life of Christianity consist. And this work is the foundation of all acceptable duties to God. Therefore, I will draw the following conclusions.

To the consternation of hypocrites and false believers, I maintain that the pains and labors which many people have taken in religion are simply lost labors—pains to no purpose that will account for nothing. Many great services and glorious works have been performed by men, which are utterly rejected by God. These works will never be on record or accepted for eternity because they were performed without any care to keep the heart with God in those duties. This is that fatal rock upon which thousands of vain, professing Christians split themselves eternally. They are curious about the externals of religion but neglectful of their hearts.

Oh, how many hours have some professing Christians spent in hearing, praying, reading, and confessing? And yet, as to the main end of religion, it would have been as good for them to have sat still and done nothing; for all this signifies nothing when the great work, heart

181

work, is all the while neglected. Tell me, vain pretender, when did you shed a tear for the deadness, hardness, unbelief, or earthliness of your heart? Do you think that such an easy religion can save you? If so, we may invert Christ's words and say wide is the gate and broad is the way that leads to life, and many there are that enter in.[1] Hear me, you self-deceiving hypocrite, you who have put off God with heartless duties, who have acted in religion as if you had been worshipping an idol that could not search and discover your heart, and who have offered to God only the skin of the sacrifice but not the marrow, fat, and meat of it: how will you abide the coming of the Lord? How will you hold up your head before Him when He will say:

Oh, you false-hearted hypocrite, how you could profess religion! With what face could you so often tell me you loved me when you knew all the while in your own conscience that your heart was not with me?

Oh, tremble to think what a fearful judgment it is to be given over to a heedless and careless heart, only using religious duties to quiet and still your conscience!

Here, I also conclude—to the shame of even upright hearts—that unless the people of God spend more time and labor on their hearts than they ordinarily do, they are never likely to do God much service or to attain much comfort in this life.

I could say of that Christian who is remiss and careless in keeping the heart, as Jacob said of Reuben, "you shall not have preeminence."[2] It grieves me to see how many Christians there are that go up and down dejected and complaining, living with a low rate of both service and

---

[1] The opposite of what Christ taught in Matthew 7:13-14.

[2] See Genesis 49:4.

comfort. And how can they expect it to be otherwise as long as they live so carelessly? Oh, how little of their time is spent in the prayer closet to search, humble, and revive their hearts?

You say that your hearts are dead, but do you wonder why they are so when you do not keep them near the Fountain of Life? If you had dieted your bodies as you have your souls, they would have been dead too. Never expect better hearts until you take more pains with them. Those who will not have the *sweat* must not expect the *sweet* of religion.

Oh, Christians! I fear your zeal and strength has run in the wrong channel. I fear most of you could take up the Church's complaint: "They made me keeper of the vineyards, but my own vineyard I have not kept!" (Song 1:6). Two things have eaten up the time and strength of the Church in this generation and sadly diverted us from heart work.

First, there have been fruitless controversies started by Satan (I don't doubt for this very purpose) to take us off from practical godliness, to make us puzzle our *heads* when we should be searching our *hearts*. Oh, how little do we remember the Apostle's teaching that "it is good for the heart to be strengthened by grace, not by foods"—with disputes and controversies about food—"which have not benefited those devoted to them" (Heb 13:9). Oh, how much better it is to see believers *live rightly* than to hear them *dispute subtly*. These unfruitful questions have divided churches, wasted time and energy, and called Christians off from their main business from looking after their own vineyard. What do you think? Would it not have been better if the questions discussed among the people of God in recent days had been ones like these:

- How can we discern the special operations of the Spirit from common ones?
- How can backsliding Christians recover their first love?

- How can our hearts be preserved from unwelcome thoughts in duty?
- How can our heart sins be discovered and mortified?

Would these questions not have done more for the credit of religion and the comfort of our souls?

Oh, it is time to repent and to be ashamed of this folly! When I read what the papist Suarez said, who wrote many volumes of disputations, that he prized the time he set apart for the searching and examining of his heart in reference to God above all the time that he ever spent in other studies, I am ashamed to find the professing Christians of this age still insensible of their folly. Will the conscience of a Suarez feel a relenting pang for wasting time and strength, and will not you? This is what your ministers have long warned you of; your spiritual nurses were afraid of the rickets when they saw your heads growing while your hearts withered. Oh, when will God beat our swords of dispute and contention into plowshares of practical godliness?

Another cause of neglecting our hearts has been earthly encumbrances. The heads and hearts of many have been so filled with the noise of worldly business that they have sadly and sensibly declined and withered in their zeal, love, and delight in God and in their ability to talk seriously and profitably about heavenly things with others.

Oh, how has this wilderness entangled us! Our discourses and conversations and even our very prayers and duties have a tang of it. We have had so much work outdoors that we have been able to do very little within. It was the sad complaint of one holy man, who said:

"Oh! It is sad to think of how many precious opportunities I have lost. How many sweet movements and admonitions of the Spirit have I passed over unfruitfully and made the Lord speak in vain in the secret entrances of His Spirit? The Lord has called upon me, but

my worldly thoughts still lodged within me, and there was no place in my heart for such calls of God!"

Surely, there is a way of enjoying God even in our worldly employments; God would never have assigned us to them to our detriment. Enoch "walked with God...and had other sons and daughters" (Gen 5:22). He walked with God, but he did not retire and separate himself from the things of this life. And the angels that are employed by Christ in the things of this world (for the spirit of the living creatures is in the wheels)[3] are finite creatures and cannot be in two places at once, yet they lose nothing of the glorious vision all the time of their administration:

"For I tell you that in heaven their angels always see the face of my Father who is in heaven." (Matt 18:10)

We need not lose our view of the Lord by our employments unless the fault is our own. Alas! Many Christians stand at the door of eternity and have more work on their hands than this poor moment of interposing time is sufficient for, yet they are filling both their heads and hearts with trifles.

I also infer—for the awakening of all—that if the keeping of the heart is the great work of a Christian, then there are very few real Christians in the world.

Many have learned the dialect of Christianity and can talk like a saint. Others have gifts and roles and by the common grace of the spirit can preach, pray, and discourse like a Christian. If everyone who associates themselves with the people of God and delights in the ordinances may pass as Christians, then the number is great.

---

[3] See Ezekiel's vision in Ezekiel 1:4-21.

But alas! How small the number shrinks to if you judge them by this rule! How few are there that conscientiously keep their hearts, watch their thoughts, and judge their ends? Oh, there are only a few closet men and women among those who profess to believe![4] It is far easier for us to be reconciled to any duties in religion than to this. The profane part of the world will not even come close to touching the external aspects of religious duties, much less with this; and though hypocrites are polite and curious about the externals, you can never persuade them to this inward and difficult work that lacks the inducement of human applause. This same work would quickly discover what hypocrites care not to know. Therefore, by a general agreement, this heart work is left in the hands of a few secret ones, and I tremble to think in how few hands it is.

Exhortation

If the keeping of the heart is such an important business; if you accrue such choice advantages by it; and if so many dear and precious blessings are wrapped up in it, then let me call upon the people of God everywhere to set quickly to this work.

Oh, study your hearts, watch your hearts, and keep your hearts. Rid yourselves of fruitless controversies and idle questions, empty titles and vain performances, unprofitable debates, and bold censures of others. Turn in upon yourselves, get into your prayer closets, and then resolve to dwell there. For too long, you have been strangers to this work, kept other vineyards, and trifled around the borders of Christianity. For too long, this world has detained you from your great work. Will you now resolve to look more to your hearts? Will you hurry and come out of the crowds of business and the clamors of the world to spend time

---

[4] Referring to individuals who spend time alone with God (i.e. in their prayer closet).

with God more than you have done? Oh, that this would be the day you would resolve to do it!

Reader, I think that I should prevail with you; all that I beg for is simply this: that you would step aside a little more often to talk with God; that you would not suffer every trifle to divert you; that you would keep a more true and faithful account of your thoughts and affections; and that you would seriously demand of your own heart, at least every evening:

> *Oh, my heart where have you been today? Where have you traveled today?*

If all that has been said by way of inducement is not enough, I have yet more motives to offer to you.

Increased spiritual understanding

The studying, observing, and diligent keeping of your own heart will marvelously help your understanding of the deep mysteries of the faith. An honest, well-examined heart is a singular help to a weak head. Such a heart will serve you in understanding a large portion of Scripture better than a commentary. By this means, you will far better understand the things of God than the learned rabbis and profound doctors (if graceless and unexperienced) ever did. You will not only have a clearer perception, but it will be sweeter and more full of life. A man may discourse correctly and profoundly on the nature and effects of faith, the troubles and comforts of conscience, and the sweetness of communion with God, without ever feeling the efficacy and sweet impressions of these things on his own spirit. But, oh, how dark and dry are these notions compared with the heart of a man on whom they have been acted?

This man reads David's psalms or Paul's epistles, and there he finds his own complaints made and answered. He says to himself:

> *Oh, these holy men speak my very heart! Their doubts are mine; their troubles are mine, and their experiences are mine.*

I remember Chrysostom speaking to his people of Antioch about some precious experiences, saying, "Those that are initiated know what I say. Experience is the best schoolmaster." Oh, then, study your hearts and keep your hearts!

Protection from prevalent errors of the day

The study and observation of your own heart will inoculate you against the dangerous and infecting errors of the times and places that you live in. Why do you think that so many professing Christians in England have departed from the faith and given heed to fables? What is the reason that so many thousands have been led away by the errors of the wicked? And why have those who have sown false doctrines had such a plentiful harvest among us? It is because they have met with a company of empty, nominal believers that never knew what belongs to practical godliness and the study of their own hearts.

If believers simply spent the time to diligently study, search, and watch their own hearts, they would have that steadfastness of their own that Peter speaks of (2 Pet 3:17).[5] And this would support and calm them (Heb 13:9).[6] Suppose a clever Papist would talk of the dignity and

---

[5] **2 Pet 3:17** "You therefore, beloved, knowing this beforehand, take care that you are not carried away with the error of lawless people and lose your own stability."

[6] **Heb 13:9** "Do not be led away by diverse and strange teachings, for it is good for the heart to be strengthened by grace, not by foods, which have not benefited those devoted to them."

merit of good works; could he ever work the persuasion of it into that heart that is conscious in itself of so much darkness, deadness, distraction, and unbelief that attends its best duties? It is a good rule that there is no argument against taste: you cannot argue against that which a man has felt and tasted.

Assurance of your salvation

Your care and diligence to keep your heart will prove to be one of the best indicators of the sincerity of your faith; for I do not know of any external act of religion that distinguishes the true professing Christian from the false one.

It is amazing to consider how far hypocrites will go in all external duties and how plausibly they can order the outward man, hiding all their indecencies from the observation of the world, but they take no heed to their hearts. They are not in secret what they appear to be in public. And before this trial, no hypocrite can stand. It is possible that in pain upon a death they may in a fit cry for the wickedness of their hearts. But alas! There is no heed to be taken to these extorted complaints, just as in our law where no credit is to be given to the testimony of one upon the rack, because it may be supposed that the severity of the torture may make the individual say anything to be eased.

However, if self-concern, care, and watchfulness be the daily work and frame of your heart, it strongly argues for the sincerity of it. For what except the sense of a divine eye and the real hatred of the sinfulness of sin could put you upon those secret duties that lie out of the observation of all creatures?

If then it is a desirable thing in your eyes to have a fair testimony of your integrity and to know for certain that you fear God, then study your heart, watch your heart, and keep your heart.

Increased joy in spiritual duties

How fruitful, sweet, and comfortable would all the ordinances and duties be to you if your heart were better kept? Oh, consider the precious communion you might have with God every time you approach Him if your heart were in tune. You might then say with David, "My meditation of him shall be sweet" (Ps 104:34, KJV). The thing that loses all your comforts in ordinances and secret duties is the reluctance of your heart. Christians whose hearts are in a good frame get a head start over others in the same duty who are tugging hard to get their hearts up to God—now trying this argument upon them and then another—to energize and affect them, and sometimes they leave as bad as they came. Sometimes the duty is almost ended before their hearts begin to stir and feel any warmth, life, or power from it. But all this while, the prepared heart is at its work; these individuals typically get the first sight of Christ in a sermon, the first seal from Christ in a sacrament, and the first kiss from Christ in secret prayer. I tell you only what I have felt—that prayers and sermons would appear differently to you than they do now if you would only bring a better-ordered heart to them. Then you would not go away dejected and drooping, saying *"Oh, this has been a lost day and a lost duty to me!"* If you had not lost your heart, it might not be so. Therefore, if you want to experience the sweet comfort of the ordinances, look to your heart, and keep your heart.

More focused prayers

Acquaintance with your own hearts can also be a fountain that supplies you in prayer. Those who are diligent in heart work and know the state of their own souls will have an overflowing fountain of praises and prayers to supply them in all their addresses to God. The tongue will not falter for something to pray.

> *"My heart overflows with a pleasing theme;*
> *I address my verses to the king;*
> *my tongue is like the pen of a ready scribe." (Ps 45:1)*

Montanus renders the original text as,

> *"My heart is boiling up good matter like a living spring that is still*
> *bubbling up fresh water; my tongue is as the pen of a ready writer."*

Others must pump their memory and rack their minds, and they are still often at a loss after all of this; but if you have kept and faithfully studied your own heart, it will be with you (as Job speaks in another case) like bottles full of new wine that want to vent and are ready to burst. And holy prayers from such a heart are not only more plentiful but also sweeter and more fervent. When you are experienced with your heart and mourn before God over a specific heart corruption or wrestle before God for the supply of some special inward need, you do not speak as others do who have learned to pray by rote; their confessions and petitions are squeezed out, but yours drop freely like pure honey from the comb. It is a happiness to be near such Christians. I remember Bernard, having given rules to prepare the heart for prayer, concludes them with the following request: *"When your heart is in this frame, then remember me."*

Recovery of spiritual power

In this way, the decaying power of Christianity will be recovered again among believers, which is the most desirable sight in this world. Oh, that I might live to see that day, when Christians will not walk in a vain show, when they will no longer please themselves with the appearance of life while being spiritually dead, and when they will no longer be (as many are now) a company of superficial, vain persons. Instead, the majestic beams of holiness will shine from their heavenly and serious speech that will awe the world and command reverence from everyone around them. And they will warm the hearts of all who come near to them so that everyone will say, "God is truly in these people." And such a time may again be expected according to Scripture:

"Your people shall all be righteous;
they shall possess the land forever,
the branch of my planting, the work of my hands,
that I might be glorified." (Isa 60:21)

But until we are more attentive to this great work of keeping our hearts, I have lost hope to see those blessed days. I cannot expect better times until God gives better hearts. Does it not grieve you to see how the world scorns the Christian faith? What objects of scorn and contempt are made of those who profess to follow Christ?

Christians, do you long to restore your credit? Would you want to obtain an honorable testimony in the consciences of your enemies? Then, keep your hearts and watch your hearts. It is the looseness, superficiality, and worldliness of your hearts that have shaped your lives, and this has brought you under the contempt of the world. You first lost sight of God and your communion with Him, and then you lost your heavenly and serious deportment among others (and by that your place in their consciences). Oh, then! For the credit of the Gospel and the honor of your testimony, keep your hearts.

Removal of stumbling blocks to faith

If we diligently keep our hearts, we will prevent and remove many of the fatal scandals and stumbling blocks out of the way of the world. Consider the warning of Christ:

"Woe to the one by whom the temptation comes." (Matt 18:7)

Do you not cover your face with shame? Does your heart not bleed within you to hear of the scandalous miscarriages of so many loose professing Christians? Could you not, like Shem and Japheth, walk backward with a garment to cover the shame of many believers?[7] How the worthy name of Christ is blasphemed (James 2:7),[8] and the hearts of the righteous are saddened (Ezek 36:20).[9] Because of this, the world is greatly prejudiced against Christ and religion, and the bonds of death are tightened on their souls. Those who began with a general love and attraction to the way of God are startled and quite driven back, and thus, soul-blood is shed. Woe to the world.

Indeed, how are the consciences of fallen professors not plunged and even overwhelmed in the depths of trouble? God inwardly excommunicates their souls from all comfortable fellowship with Himself and the joys of His salvation. Infinite damage is done by the scandalous lives of professing Christians.

---

[7] A reference to Genesis 9:23 when Shem and Japheth walked backward with a garment to cover the nakedness of their sleeping father, Noah.

[8] **James 2:7** "Are they not the ones who blaspheme the honorable name by which you were called?"

[9] **Ezek 36:20** "But when they came to the nations, wherever they came, they profaned my holy name, in that people said of them, 'These are the people of the Lord, and yet they had to go out of his land.'"

And what is the true cause and reason for all of this but the neglecting of our hearts? If our hearts were better kept, all of this would be prevented. Had David kept his *heart*, he would not have broken his *bones*.[10] A neglected, careless heart must necessarily produce a disordered, scandalous life. I thank God for the freedom and faithfulness of a reverend brother in showing Christians their manifold miscarriages![11] I sincerely wish from my heart that after their wounds have been thoroughly searched by that probe, God would be pleased to heal them by this treatment. Oh, professors! If you are ever to keep religion sweet and if you ever hope to recover your testimony in the world, keep your hearts! Either keep your hearts or lose your testimony. Keep your hearts or lose your comforts. Keep your hearts lest you shed the blood of souls. What words can express the deep importance and the wonderful consequences of this work? Everything reveals it to be necessary, serious, and beautiful.

Preparation for the future

A well-kept heart will fit you for any condition that God casts you into or any service He has planned for you. The one who has learned how to keep the heart humble is fit for prosperity, and the one who knows how to use and apply the promises and supports of Scripture is fit to pass through any adversity. If you can deny the pride and selfishness of your heart, you are fit to be employed in any service for God. Paul was such a man; he did not only spend his time preaching to others—keeping other vineyards—but he also looked to himself and kept his own vineyards:

---

[10] See David's lament over his sin in Psalm 51.

[11] *A Gospel Glass,* Lewis Stuckley.

"But I discipline my body and keep it under control, lest after preaching to others I myself should be disqualified." (1 Cor 9:27)

And what an eminent instrument Paul was for God. He could turn his hand to any work, knowing how to skillfully manage both an adverse and prosperous condition (Phil 4:12).[12] Let the people defy him; it does not move him (unless it is to indignation). Let them stone him; he can bear it.

"Therefore, if anyone cleanses himself from what is dishonorable, he will be a vessel for honorable use, set apart as holy, useful to the master of the house, ready for every good work." (2 Tim 2:21)

First, your heart must be purged, and then it is prepared for any service to God. When the heart of Isaiah was purified—which was signified by the touching of his lips with a coal from the altar—then he was fit for God's work: "Here I am! Send me" (Isa 6:8). Consider a man who has not learned to keep his heart. If you give him any service for God that is attended with honor, it will swell up his spirit in pride. If you give him suffering, it will depress and sink him.

Jesus Christ was more fit for the Father's work than any servant that God ever employed. He was zealous in public work for God—so zealous that He sometimes forgot to eat bread, and His friends thought He was beside Himself. However, He conducted Himself this way in His public work without forgetting His own private communion with God. We see in Matthew 14:23 that after a day of labor, He went up to a mountain alone to pray. Oh, let the keepers of the vineyards look to

---

[12] **Phil 4:12** "I know how to be brought low, and I know how to abound. In any and every circumstance, I have learned the secret of facing plenty and hunger, abundance and need."

their own vineyards! We will never be so instrumental to the good of others as when we are most diligent about our own souls.

Closer fellowship with other believers

If the people of God would more diligently keep their hearts, consider how the fellowship of saints would be exceedingly sweetened! How lovely then would be your tents, O Jacob, and your encampments, O Israel (Num 24:5). Or as it is prophesied of the Jews:

"Let us go with you, for we have heard that God is with you."
(Zech 8:23)

It is the fellowship that your souls have with the Father and with the Son that draws others to want to fellowship with you (1 John 1:3).[13] I tell you, if saints would be persuaded to make more effort and spend more time with their hearts, there could quickly be such a divine luster on the face of their conversations that others would consider it no small privilege to be near them.

It is the pride, passion, and earthliness of our hearts that have spoiled Christian fellowship. Why are Christians often jarring and contentious when they meet? Is it not from their unmortified passions? Where do their uncharitable judgments of their brothers and sisters arise from? Is it not from self-ignorance? Why are they so rigid and unmerciful toward those who have fallen? Is it not from their refusal to

---

[13] **1 John 1:3** "That which we have seen and heard we proclaim also to you, so that you too may have fellowship with us; and indeed our fellowship is with the Father and with his Son Jesus Christ."

consider their own weaknesses, as the apostle speaks (Gal 6:1)?[14] Why is their discourse so shallow and unprofitable when they meet? Is it not from the earthliness and vanity of their hearts?

My friends, these are the things that have spoiled Christian fellowship, making it so dry and sapless that many Christians are even weary of it and are ready to say with past saints:

> *"Oh that I had in the desert a travelers' lodging place, that I might leave my people and go away from them!" (Jer 9:2)*

> *"Too long have I had my dwelling among those who hate peace." (Ps 120:6)*

This has made them long for the grave, that they might go from those who are not their own people to the ones who are their own people (as the original text of 2 Cor 5:8[15] implies).

But now, if professing believers would study, watch, and keep their hearts better, all this would be prevented, and the beauty and glory of fellowship would again be restored. We would no longer divide, conflict, or rashly judge. If our hearts were in tune, our tongues would not jar. How charitable, compassionate, and tender we would be to one another if we were daily humbled under the evil of our own hearts. May the Lord hasten the day when we have this type of fellowship, and may He bless these counsels to aid it in coming.

---

[14] **Gal 6:1** "Brothers, if anyone is caught in any transgression, you who are spiritual should restore him in a spirit of gentleness. Keep watch on yourself, lest you too be tempted."

[15] **2 Cor 5:8** "Yes, we are of good courage, and we would rather be away from the body and at home with the Lord."

Increased benefit from spiritual duties

Lastly, by keeping your heart, the comforts of the Spirit and the precious influences of all the ordinances would be established and much longer preserved in your soul than they are now. Ah! What would I give for my soul to be preserved in the frame that I sometimes find it in after an ordinance! Sometimes, Oh Lord, (said one of the fathers sweetly) You admit me into the most inward, unusual, and sweet delights to I know not what sweetness, which if it were perfected in me, I do not know what it would be, or rather, what it would not be. But alas! The heart grows careless again and quickly returns, like water removed from the stove, to its native coldness. If you could only keep those things forever in your hearts, what Christians would you be! What lives would you live!

But how is it that these things do not remain longer with us? Doubtless, it is because we allow our hearts to become cold again. We should be as careful after an ordinance or spiritual duty to prevent this as one that comes out of a hot bath is of going into the chill air. We have our hot and cold fits in their turns, and what is the reason but our unskillfulness and carelessness in keeping the heart.

It is a thousand pities that the ordinances of God, as to their energizing and comforting effects, should be like those human ordinances the apostle speaks of that perish in the using.[16] Oh then, let me say to you: "Are the comforts of God too small for you" (Job 15:11)? Look over these ten special benefits and weigh them on just scales. Are they small matters? Is it a small matter to have your weak understanding assisted, your endangered soul cured, your sincerity cleared, your communion with God sweetened, and your sails filled in prayer? Is it a small thing to have the decaying power of godliness again restored, to have all fatal scandals removed, to gain an instrumental fitness for serving

---

[16] Referring to Colossians 2:20-22.

Christ, to restore the communion of saints to its original glory, and to have the influences of the ordinances abiding in the souls of saints? If these are no common blessings or small benefits, then surely it is a great duty to keep the heart with all diligence.

Chapter 16

Final Directions

The next use for this teaching provides directions on some special means to keep the heart. These complement what has been hinted at in the explanation of the duty in chapter one and in the other directions in this book about different seasons of life. Here, I will add several other general guidelines that are of excellent use for this end.

Live in the Word

Do you want to keep your heart as it has been argued here? Then furnish your heart richly with the Word of God, which is your best preservative against sin. Keep the Word, and the Word will keep you. Just as first receiving the Word regenerates your heart, so keeping the Word within you will preserve your heart:

> *"Let the word of Christ dwell in you richly, teaching and admonishing one another in all wisdom, singing psalms and hymns and spiritual songs, with thankfulness in your hearts to God." (Col 3:16)*

Let it dwell richly, or plentifully, in all that it contains (its commands, promises, and warnings) in all that is in you (your understanding, memory, conscience, and affections). Then it will preserve your heart.

> *"I have stored up your word in my heart, that I might not sin against you." (Ps 119:11)*

The slipperiness of our hearts with respect to the Word is the cause of so many slips in our lives. Conscience cannot be urged or awed with forgotten truths; but keep them in the heart, and they will keep both heart and life upright.

> *"The law of his God is in his heart;*
> *his steps do not slip." (Ps 37:31)*

Or, if he does slip, the Word will recover the straying heart again. "And Peter remembered the saying of Jesus…And he went out and wept bitterly" (Matt 26:75). We never lose our hearts until they have first lost the efficacious and powerful impression of the Word.

Question your heart

Frequently call your heart to account if you ever intend to keep it with God. Those that put responsibilities into the hands of unfaithful or suspicious servants will be sure to make short reckonings with them.

> *"The heart is deceitful above all things,*
> *and desperately sick;*
> *who can understand it?" (Jer 17:9)*

Oh, it is as necessary as it is sweet that we and our secret thoughts should confer together every night (Ps 16:7).[1] We should call our hearts to account every evening and say:

Oh, my heart! Where have you been today? Where have your thoughts wandered today? What account can you give of them? Oh, disobedient heart, vain heart, could you not abide by the fountain of delights? Is there better entertainment with the creature than with God?

The more often our hearts meet with rebukes and checks for wandering, the less they will wander. If every vain thought were retracted with a sigh and if every excursion of the heart from God were met with a severe check, we would not dare so boldly and frequently to digress and step aside. The actions that are committed with reluctance are not committed with frequency.

Make room for God

If you desire to keep your heart, you must be careful of plunging yourself into such a multiplicity of earthly business so as to be unable to manage without neglecting your main business. It is impossible to imagine how you can keep your heart with God if you have lost yourself in a forest of earthly business. Take care that you do not pinch your soul by gratifying the immoderate desires of your flesh. I wish many Christians could truly say what a heathen once did, "I do not give but only lend myself to my business." It is said Germanicus reigned in the

---

[1] **Ps 16:7** "I bless the Lord who gives me counsel; in the night also my heart instructs me."

Romans' hearts but Tiberius only in their provinces. Though the world is in your hands, do not let it jostle Christ out of your heart.

Take heed Christian lest your *shop* steals away your heart from your *closet*.[2] God never intended earthly employments for a *stop* but rather for a *step* to heavenly ones. Oh, let not Aristippus the heathen arise in judgment against you when he said that he would rather neglect his means than his mind and his farm than his soul. If your ship is over-laden, you must cast some cargo overboard. More business than you can well manage is like more meat than you can well digest: it will quickly make you sick.

Watch for warning signs

If you mean to keep your heart, you must carefully observe its first backslidings from God, and stop it there. A man who wants his house to be in good repair must stop up every crack as soon as it is discovered, and he who would keep his heart must not let a vain thought be long neglected. Apostasy, the serpent of the heart, is best killed as an egg of a small backsliding. Oh, if many poor decayed Christians had looked to their hearts in time, they would never have ended up in the sad condition they currently find themselves in. We may say of heart-neglect as the apostle does of vain babblings—that "it will lead people into more and more ungodliness" (2 Tim 2:16). Little sins neglected will quickly become great uncontrollable ones. The greatest crocodile once lay in an egg, and the greatest oak was once only an acorn. The lighting of a small amount of gun powder may blow up all by leading to a greater quantity. People think very little about what a proud, vain, lustful, or worldly thought may grow to be. Behold how great a matter is kindled by a small fire.

---

[2] A reference to worldly business (i.e. your shop) versus spiritual life (i.e. your prayer closet).

Stay close to God

Take care not to lose the vitality and sweetness of your communion with God lest, thereby, your hearts are loosed off from God. The heart is a hungry and restless thing; it will have something to feed upon. If it enjoys nothing from God, it will hunt for something among the creation, and there it often loses itself as well as its purpose. There is nothing that more engages the heart to be steadfast and faithful in walking with God than the sweetness which it tastes therein. It is like the Gauls; after they had tasted the sweet wine of Italy, they could never be satisfied until they conquered the country where it grew.

Certainly, conscientiousness in duty may keep the heart from neglecting it, but when there is no higher motive, it drives forward listlessly and is filled with distractions. That which we delight in we are never weary of, which is evident in the motions of the heart to earthly things, whose wheels run nimbly when oiled with delight. The motions of our hearts upward would run more freely if our delight in heavenly things were greater.

Meditate

Habituate your heart to spiritual meditations if you would have it freed from those burdensome diversions. By this means, you will gain an ability and dexterity in heart-work. It is a pity those smaller portions of our time between solemn duties should lie in our hands and be rendered useless to us. Oh, learn to save, and be good caretakers of your thoughts. To this purpose, an astute author once said:[3]

"These parentheses that happen to come between the more solemn passages (whether business or recreation) of human life are likely to

---

[3] *Occasional Reflections,* Robert Boyle.

be lost by most believers because they lack an appropriate value for them. And even by good men for want of skill to preserve them. For though they do not properly despise them, yet they neglect or lose them for lack of knowing how to rescue them or what to do with them. But, although grains of sand and ashes are apart and uselessly small so as to be liable to be scattered and blown away, yet the skill-ful craftsman, by a vehement fire, brings many of these together to afford him that noble substance of glass. And glass allows us to both see ourselves and our blemishes clearly represented (as in a mirror) and to discern celestial objects (as with a telescope) and with sun-beams light burnable materials (as with a magnifying glass). So when these little fragments or parcels of time, which if not carefully looked to would be dissipated and lost, come to be managed by a skillful contemplator and to be improved by the celestial fire of de-votion, they may be so ordered as to afford us both looking glasses to dress our souls at and insights to discover heavenly wonders and incentives to inflame our hearts with zeal."

I have something similar that I am working on for the public good, if God gives me life to finish it and the opportunity to produce it. Cer-tainly, this is a great advantage for keeping the heart with God.

Chapter 17

Comfort for Struggling Saints

I will now close the whole with a word or two of comfort to all the diligent and serious Christians who faithfully and closely apply this heart-work; who are groaning and weeping in secret over the hardness, pride, worldliness, and vanity of their hearts; and who are fearing and trembling over the falseness of them. Meanwhile, other vain professing Christians' eyes are focused outward, their time and strength are eaten up by fruitless disputes, worldly employments, or at best by cold and formal performances of some heartless and empty duties. Poor Christian, I have three things to offer you for your support and comfort, and I have no doubt that either of them alone, when mixed with faith, is sufficient to comfort you over all the trouble you have with your own heart.

Your heart matters more than your abilities

No matter what your other gifts and abilities, your attitude argues that your heart is upright and honest. An upright heart will comfort you on a death bed.

"'Now, O Lord, please remember how I have walked before you in faithfulness and with a whole heart, and have done what is good in your sight.' And Hezekiah wept bitterly." (2 Kings 20:3)

I wholeheartedly agree with the one who said, "If I had my wish, I would prefer the lowliest work of a poor Christian, before all the victories and triumphs of Alexander or Cesar" (and I would add before all the extensive duties and excellent gifts of false believers or the tongues of men and angels). It will add more to my comfort to spend one solitary hour in the morning before the Lord over heart corruption than many hours in a seemingly zealous, but really dead, performance of common duties with the greatest acclaim and richest embellishments of abilities and gifts.

By this very thing, Christ distinguishes the formal and serious Christian (Matt 6:5).[1] The one is in the street and Synagogue to receive the eyes and applause of men; the other is at home in his closet to work on his heart. Therefore, never be troubled then for the lack of the things that a man may have and be eternally damned. But rather, bless God for that which none but the favorites and darlings of heaven have. Many are now in hell that had a better head than yours, and many are now in heaven that complained of a heart as bad as yours.

God is working for your good

Furthermore, be comforted by the truth that God would never leave you under so many heart troubles and burdens if He did not actually intend them for your benefit. You are often crying out like this:

---

[1] **Matt 6:5** "And when you pray, you must not be like the hypocrites. For they love to stand and pray in the synagogues and at the street corners, that they may be seen by others. Truly, I say to you, they have received their reward."

Lord, why is it this way? Why do I go mourning all day, having sorrow in my heart? See how long I have been exercised with hardness of heart, and to this day, I have not obtained a submissive heart. Many years I have been praying and striving against vain thoughts, yet I am still infected and perplexed with them. Oh, when will I get a better heart! I have been working hard but brought forth only wind. I have obtained no deliverance, neither have the corruptions of my heart fallen. I have brought this heart many times to prayers, sermons, and sacraments, expecting and hoping for a cure from my corruptions, and still my sore runs without ceasing.

Pensive soul, let this comfort you: God is working for your good, even by these occasions of your sad complaints. For through these, He helps you to see what your heart is and was by nature and therein to acknowledge how much you owe to free grace! He leaves you under these exercises of the Spirit that you may lie as with your face upon the ground, admiring that the Lord of Glory should ever have taken such a toad, so vile a creature, into His bosom. Your base heart, if it is good for nothing else, yet serves to commend and bring out the unsearchable riches of free grace. This serves to keep you from continually resting or even glancing upon your own righteousness or excellence; the corruption of your heart, working in all your duties makes you sensible to feel that the bed is too short and the covering too narrow. Were it not for those meditations you have after spiritual duties on the dullness and distractions of your heart in them, how apt would you be to fall in love with and admire your own performances and increases? For if even with these duties you have much work to do with the pride of your heart, how much more if such humbling and self-abasing considerations were lacking?

And lastly, this tends to make you more compassionate and tender toward others. Perhaps you would have little pity for the distresses and soul-troubles of others if you had less experience of your own.

Complete rest is near

To conclude, God will shortly put a blessed end to all these troubles, cares, and labors. The time is coming when your heart will be as you desire; when you will be discharged of these cares, fears, and sorrows and never again cry out, *"Oh, my hard, proud, vain, earthly heart!"*; when all darkness will be banished from your understanding and you will clearly discover all truths in God, that crystal ocean of truth; and when you will be perfectly purged of all corruptions. Then your thoughts will be everlastingly, ravishingly, and delightfully entertained and exercised upon that supreme goodness and infinite excellency of God, from Whom they will never recoil like a broken bow. And as for your pride, passion, worldliness, and all other subjects of your complaints and troubles, let it be said of them as of the Egyptians to Israel:

> *"Fear not, stand firm, and see the salvation of the Lord." (Exodus 14:13)*

These corruptions you see today, henceforth you will see them no more forever! Soon you will lay down your weapons of prayers, tears, and groans, and you will put on the armor of light—not to fight but to triumph!

Lord, when will this blessed day come? How long? How long? Holy and True, my soul waits for you!

"Make haste, my beloved,
and be like a gazelle
or a young stag
on the mountains of spices."
(Song 8:14)

Amen.

Made in the USA
Middletown, DE
05 September 2024

60434260R00117